# navy's Most Wanted™

## The Top 10 Book of Admirable Admirals, Sleek Submarines, and Oceanic Oddities

**Norman Polmar**

and

**Christopher P. Cavas**

Potomac Books, Inc.
WASHINGTON, D.C.

**Library of Congress Cataloging-in-Publication Data**

Polmar, Norman.
Navy's most wanted : the top 10 book of admirable admirals, sleek submarines, and oceanic oddities / Norman Polmar and Christopher P. Cavas. — 1st ed.
p. cm.
Includes bibliographical references and index.
ISBN 978-1-59797-226-0 (pbk. : alk. paper)
1. United States—History, Naval—Miscellanea. 2. United States. Navy—History—Miscellanea. 3. United States. Navy—Biography—Miscellanea. I. Cavas, Christopher P. II. Title.
E182.P76 2009
359.00973—dc22

2008039380

Printed in the United States of America on acid-free paper that meets the American National Standards Institute Z39-48 Standard.

Potomac Books, Inc.
22841 Quicksilver Drive
Dulles, Virginia 20166

First Edition

10 9 8 7 6 5 4 3 2 1

# Contents

# Contents

# Illustrations

# Preface

Much history, myth, and technology, as well as fascinating personalities inundate the records of navies—which date back to antiquity. While it is impossible to determine when or where primitive people first used a floating vessel as a fighting platform, or to transport soldiers, there is evidence that such vessels have existed for perhaps five and a half millennium.

Naval historians Donald Macintyre and Basil W. Bathe wrote in their landmark study *Man-of-War* in 1969:

> Drawings of ships carrying tribal standards on Egyptian vases of the period before 3400 B.C. are possibly the earliest extant representations of ships of war. These crude drawings—some authorities even doubt that they represent ships—appear to show river craft, about fifty feet in length, with cabins amidships.
>
> Other vases of about the same date from southern Egypt show for the first time a sail, and a steering oar used over the stern quarter of the vessel.

From the earliest beginnings came the oared and then sailing ships—carrying troops and then cannon, too—that initially powered by sail, then by steam engines, drawing their energy from coal, then oil, and eventually nuclear fission. And, not only did navies sail on the surface of the seas, but early in the 20th Century navies were flying over the seas in aircraft and lighter-than-air airships, and moving under the seas in submarines. Today missiles and satellites complement these vessels and vehicles as they carry out their missions in peacetime as well as in crises and conflicts.

*Navy's Most Wanted*™ provides a series of snapshots of this long and convoluted development of navies. Some entries are serious, some whimsical, and some simply fun. Most important are the people—both in uniform and in mufti—be they heroes or villains (such as pirates).

The authors have, obviously, often selected their favorites although some attempt was made at objectivity. The entries about people who went to sea are our favorites, plus a few who have not gone "down to the sea in ships" but have had a major impact on those who did and their ships. Foremost among the latter were Theodore Roosevelt, Franklin D. Roosevelt, and Winston Churchill.

While it is difficult, nay, impossible to choose the most significant ship, or naval aircraft, or naval officer, or politician mentioned in *Navy's Most Wanted*™, without a doubt the most influential, longest serving, most prolific writer, and most quoted person is Churchill—who described himself as a "former naval person." For many people his most important contribution to naval history was his oft cited description of one of the most important navies of all time: "The traditions of the Royal Navy . . . rum, buggery, and the lash."

While those traditions are not addressed in this book, we hope that the many that are cited will be of interest—and entertainment—to our readers.

# Quotations

1. **SKILL IN NAVAL AFFAIRS, AS IN OTHER CRAFTS, IS THE RESULT OF SCIENTIFIC TRAINING. IT IS IMPOSSIBLE TO ACQUIRE THIS SKILL UNLESS THE MATTER BE TREATED AS THE FIRST IMPORTANCE AND ALL OTHER PURSUITS ARE CONSIDERED TO BE SECONDARY TO IT.**
Thucydides in his *History of the Peloponnesian Wars* (c. 404 BCE).

2. **A MAN-OF-WAR IS THE BEST AMBASSADOR.**
Oliver Cromwell.

3. **I HAVE NOT YET BEGUN TO FIGHT.**
John Paul Jones during the battle of his ship, the *Bonhomme Richard*, with the British *Serapis*, when the latter's commanding officer, Capt. Richard Pearson, asked if Jones had struck his colors (1775). Another favorite statement by Jones that warrants attention is: "I wish to have no Connection with any Ship that does not Sail fast for I intend to go in harm's way"— Jones in a letter to le Ray de Chaumont (1778).

### 4. IT FOLLOWS THEN AS CERTAIN AS NIGHT SUCCEEDS DAY, THAT WITHOUT A DECISIVE NAVAL FORCE WE CAN DO NOTHING DEFINITIVE, AND WITH IT EVERYTHING HONORABLE AND GLORIOUS.

George Washington in a letter to the Marquis de Lafayette (1781).

### 5. ENGLAND EXPECTS EVERY MAN TO DO HIS DUTY.

Vice-Adm. Horatio Nelson's signal to the ships of the British fleet closing with the France-Spanish force at the Battle of Trafalgar (1805).

### 6. DON'T GIVE UP THE SHIP!

Capt. James Lawrence after being mortally wounded in the engagement between his ship, the U.S. frigate *Chesapeake*, and HMS *Shannon* (1813). As the wounded Lawrence was carried below, he ordered: "Tell the men to fire faster! Don't give up the ship!"

### 7. WE HAVE MET THE ENEMY AND THEY ARE OURS.

Commo. Oliver Hazard Perry's dispatch to Maj. Gen. William Henry Harrison after the Battle of Lake Erie (1813).

### 8. DAMN THE TORPEDOES . . . FULL SPEED AHEAD.

Rear Adm. David Glasgow Farragut aboard his flagship *Hartford* as Union naval forces entered Mobile Bay, Alabama (1864). By "torpedoes" he meant naval mines.

### 9. YOU MAY FIRE WHEN YOU ARE READY, GRIDLEY.

Commo. George Dewey to Capt. C.V. Gridley aboard his flagship *Olympia* as his ships were about to engage the Spanish fleet at Manila Bay (1898).

**10. WHOEVER DESIGNED THAT SHIP MUST HAVE BEEN PISS-ARSE DRUNK.**
Chief Engine Room Artificer Watts, discussing HMS *Compass Rose*, a Flower-class corvette, in Nicholas Monsarrat's classic novel *The Cruel Sea* (1951).

# Inventions

navies have benefited from a host of inventions. The following are among the more significant ones.

## 1. STEAM PROPULSION

Steam propulsion permitted warships to travel and maneuver regardless of wind condition and direction. Thomas Newcomen invented the first steam engine in 1712 to pump water from coal mines. Others soon made improvements to Newcomen's design, and several inventors developed model steam-propelled craft, and by the late 1780s commercial steamboats were being built, including Robert Fulton's *Claremont* (1807). The first military use of a steamship was as a dredger in British harbors in 1802. In the War of 1812, the U.S. Army pressed a Mississippi River paddle steamer into service as a troopship. The War of 1812 also saw the construction of the first steam-powered warship, the *Demologos,* to a Fulton design. The ship was an innovative design, with a paddle wheel on the inside, sandwiched between two wooden hulls. She carried 26 32-pounder guns. But she was not completed until 1815, when the war was over. The first paddle steamer built for the Royal Navy, the *Comet* of 238 tons launched in 1822, and several similar ships that followed were not armed until about

1830. That was the same year that the French Navy acquired its first steam vessel, the *Sphinx*. The first real British steam warship was the sloop *Gorgon*, launched in 1837 and armed with two cannons. A larger steam frigate, the *Firebrand*, was launched in 1842. By the time of the American Civil War, all navies were operating steam warships.

## 2. METAL SHIPS

Metal ships—iron and, subsequently, steel—provided many advantages over wooden warships, especially being more resistant to gunfire. In addition, metal ship hulls could be shaped for optimum speeds and could carry heavier machinery and weapons. And, metal hulls were more resistant to the marine growth that slowed wooden hull ships. (During the 1700s warship hulls were sheathed in copper to resist marine growth.) The world's first iron-hulled warship was the relatively large *Warrior* of 9,210 tons (40 guns), launched in December 1860. Four months after the *Warrior*, the French Navy launched the *Couronne* of 6,428 tons (36 guns). These ships had steam engines with screw propellers—and a full set of masts and sails. In 1862 the U.S. Navy launched the similar but smaller *New Ironsides* of 4,120 tons (16 guns). (When that ship engaged Confederate Fort Sumter during the American Civil War, the *New Ironsides* survived some 60 to 70 hits on her 4-inch armor without suffering serious damage. Later a Confederate spar torpedo exploded against her hull and caused leaks and some internal damage, but she remained afloat.) Warships constructed of steel soon replaced the iron ships.

## 3. SUBMARINE

The development of a successful undersea craft—that was first proposed by British mathematician and gunner William Bourne in his *Inventions or Devices* (1578)—was made possible in the 1880s by the development of practical electric storage batteries, which could permit practical underwater propulsion by electric motors. The early pioneers included James Ash and Andrew Campbell in England, Gustave Zédé in France, Isaac Peral in Spain, and competitors John P. Holland and Simon Lake in the United States. Both Lake—probably the most innovative of his contemporaries—and Holland produced designs that were soon employed by navies around the world.

### 4. TORPEDO

In the late 1800s there were several efforts to develop self-propelled or "automobile" torpedoes. Self-propelled torpedoes provided potent ship-killing weapons for submarines, surface ships, and aircraft; they were especially effective because they tore open the underwater hull of a ship. The most successful of these early efforts were the weapons developed by Robert Whitehead, the English manager of a marine engine factory at Fiume, Austria. Whitehead sold rights to manufacture his torpedoes to several nations. His first torpedo launched in action was in 1877, when the British cruiser *Shah* launched the weapon against the Peruvian monitor *Huascar*—without effect. History was made in January 1878 when a torpedo launched by the Russian steamer *Constantine* off Batoum, Turkey, sank a Turkish steamer. In the United States Whitehead torpedoes were adopted, but several innovative designs by Americans were also evaluated and produced, among them the designs of John Ericsson (of *Monitor* fame), Comdr. C.F. Goodrich, and Capt. John A. Howell.

### 5. RADAR

Radar—an acronym for Radio Detection And Ranging—provided the means of "seeing" objects at night, in bad weather, and through smoke; in clear weather it extended the range of sight. It could detect aircraft and ships by the reflection of radio waves from solid objects. The United States, Britain, France, and Germany all developed radar in the 1930s. The first radar fitted in a warship was an experimental set installed in the U.S. Navy destroyer *Leary* (DD 158) in 1937. Early the following year, that set, attached to a gun mount, detected an aircraft at a distance of 100 miles. The more capable XAF radar was installed in the battleship *New York* (BB 34) in December 1938. That radar—with a 17-foot rotating "bed spring" antenna—and the competitive CXZ set fitted in the battleship *Texas* (BB 35) were an outstanding success in exercises, detecting aircraft and surface ships, providing excellent navigation aids in coastal waters, and spotting the fall of shots. Radar was subsequently fitted in all warships as well as in aircraft to search out surface ships as well as other aircraft. Radar had an important role in many of the U.S. and British naval successes of World War II.

## 6. PROXIMITY FUZE

The American-developed proximity fuze detonated an antiaircraft shell at the closest point of approach to an enemy aircraft. Also called an influence fuze or Variable-Time (VT) fuze, the proximity fuze greatly increased the probability that a shell would destroy an enemy aircraft. Previous "smart" fuzes that detonated at a pre-set altitude had to be set before the gun was fired and could not allow for the target aircraft's changes in speed, altitude, and direction. In mid-1940 the U.S. Navy decided that an electronic proximity fuze was practical, this belief being based in part on major British orders with a U.S. firm for magnetrons (small valves) for use in radar sets. By early 1943 some 5,000 rounds of proximity-fuze ammunition had been rushed to the South Pacific. The first combat use came on January 5, 1943, when the U.S. cruiser *Helena* (CL 50) shot down a Japanese dive bomber near New

Georgia with only a few rounds of VT ammunition. Subsequently, proximity-fuze ammunition was provided to warships in the Atlantic and Mediterranean. These rounds proved to be three times as effective as time-fuzed ammunition. The initial use was in 5-inch (127-mm) ammunition with guns of that size being mounted in all U.S. aircraft carriers, battleships, cruisers, and destroyers.

## 7. NUCLEAR PROPULSION

Nuclear propulsion freed submarines from the need to periodically surface or extend a snorkel (breathing tube) above the water to pull in air to run diesel engines in order to recharge electric storage batteries. The U.S. Navy initiated a nuclear propulsion program at the Naval Research Laboratory in Washington, D.C., in 1939. That program was put aside during World War II but was immediately reinstated when the conflict ended. The Navy led the nation's effort to develop non-weapon use of nuclear energy. Capt. Hyman G. Rickover led a Navy team sent to the nuclear facility at Oak Ridge, Tennessee. He was then named head of the Navy's nascent nuclear-propulsion program. These efforts resulted in the USS *Nautilus* (SSN 571)—the world's first nuclear "vehicle"—going to sea in January 1955. The Soviet Navy put its first nuclear submarine, the *K-3* (NATO codename November), to sea 3½ years after the *Nautilus*.

## 8. GUIDED MISSILES

Guided missiles—for several roles—provide a longer-range, more-potent, and more-accurate striking power than do shipboard guns. The first practical, long-range (150-mile) guided or cruise missile was the German V-1 "buzz bomb," which was first launched against England in June 1944. After the war the Soviet Union and United States both exploited German technology to develop cruise missiles for use against surface ships and land targets. The U.S. fleet-type submarine *Cusk* (SS 348) on February 12, 1947, launched a Loon missile (U.S. version of the V-1) while operating on the surface off the coast of California—the world's first launch of a guided missile from a submarine. Meanwhile, development was underway on a larger, more-capable Regulus cruise missile that could carry a nuclear warhead for use against ships or land targets. That weapon became operational in 1955, being fitted to submarines, cruisers, and aircraft carriers. The Soviet Navy similarly developed multi-role cruise missiles with the P-5 (NATO codename Shaddock) becoming operational in submarines and cruisers in 1959. Improved missiles were developed that could also be launched by submerged submarines. The U.S. and Soviet navies also developed surface-to-air missiles, also based in part on German technologies.

## 9. STEAM CATAPULT

The World War II-era hydraulic catapults had insufficient energy to launch the heavy post-war aircraft. Aircraft carriers had flush-deck catapult tracks fitted into the flight deck. The Royal Navy, which had pioneered the development of aircraft carriers in World War I, conceived the idea of employing steam generated by a carrier's boilers to power catapults. The steam catapult, proposed by Comdr. Colin C. Mitchell, was first installed in the British light carrier *Perseus* in 1949–1950. After successful trials with British aircraft, the carrier demonstrated the steam catapult for the U.S. Navy in 1951. The U.S. Navy immediately adopted the device, with the USS *Hancock* (CVA 19) being the first U.S. carrier to go to sea with a steam catapult in 1954.

## 10. ANGLED FLIGHT DECK

As aircraft landed aboard aircraft carriers, steel arresting wires stretched across the after section of the flight deck stopped them. A wire barrier was set up forward of the arresting wires to stop aircraft that missed the wires from smashing into aircraft parked on the forward portion of the flight deck. The advent of jet-propelled aircraft with high landing speeds in the early 1950s greatly increased the danger of landing aircraft aboard ship. The concept of an angled or canted landing deck was born in a conference at the Royal Aircraft Establishment in August 1951 as the Royal Navy's leading aviators and aeronautical engineers studied the problems of operating heavy, high-performance aircraft from carriers. Capt. Dennis R.F. Cambell proposed a ten-degree offset landing area. With the angled landing area, an aircraft that missed the arresting wires could accelerate and take off again rather than crash into a barrier or into the aircraft parked at the forward end of the flight deck. In February 1952, the light carrier *Triumph* had an angled-deck layout painted on her existing flight deck. Aircraft flew touch-and-go landings on the *Triumph*'s angled deck in mid-February. Based on this experience, a short time later similar touch-and-go landings were flown on board the larger U.S. carrier *Midway* (CVA 41), whose deck was painted with an angled landing area. In the fall of 1952 the USS *Antietam* (CVA 36) was converted to the world's first angled-deck carrier. Her landing area was angled eight degrees to port with her arresting wires being oriented to the angled deck. She demonstrated the angled-deck concept for U.S. Navy officials and then crossed the Atlantic for similar demonstrations in British waters. The angled-deck concept was immediately accepted in carrier aviation.

# Pirates

The pirates who cruised the Spanish Main still stir the imagi-nation—and the recent success of the film series *The Pirates of the Caribbean* only serves to point to the strength of the legends. Not all the scurvy dogs listed below earned their fame in the Caribbean, but all spent at least some of their sailing days there. Some might also question this list appear-ing in a "naval" history book, but all of these fugitives were chased by or served in the navies of Britain, France, Spain or the United States.

## 1. FRANCIS LE CLERC

This French corsair's nickname is recognizable to many pi-rate enthusiasts: the Spanish called him "Pie de Palo," or Peg Leg. Le Clerc lost his leg fighting the English, but he made his name fighting the Spanish. One of the first pirates on the Span-ish Main, by 1553 he was leading pirate ships and French royal warships in raids on Spanish-controlled Puerto Rico and Hispaniola, and he even hit Las Palmas in the Canary Islands. The following year he took Santiago de Cuba, Spain's capital in Cuba. In 1562 he fought for the English against French Protestants and asked Queen Elizabeth I for a pension. When

Elizabeth refused, a sulky Le Clerc went back to hunting Spanish treasure ships, but was soon killed in the Azores.

## 2. SIR FRANCIS DRAKE

Pirate, privateer, and master of court intrigue, Francis Drake was one of the first larger-than-life naval legends in Western culture. One of the captains of the victorious English fleet during the attempted invasion of 1588 by the Spanish Armada, he had gone to sea as a young lad and captained merchant ships in the New World. Queen Elizabeth gave him letters of marque in 1577 to wage war against the Spanish, and in his flagship *Golden Hinde* he sailed around South America and up what would become the California coast. Drake captured enough Spanish booty that when he returned home in 1580, the Queen's share was greater than all her other income. The problem in all this was that England and Spain were not at war; Elizabeth therefore declared all of Drake's activities to be state secrets. A hero in England, Drake was considered the worst of all pirates by the Spanish. When Spain and England went to war in 1585, Sir Francis returned to the New World for a new round of sacking and plundering. After the glories of the Armada, Drake never stopped fighting Spaniards, but lost his golden touch in a series of Caribbean defeats in 1595. He died at sea of sickness in 1596.

## 3. SIR HENRY MORGAN

Like Drake, Henry Morgan was as much "legal" privateer as a pirate, fighting under English letters of marque against the Spanish in the New World. In 1667 he captured the Spanish fortress at Porto Bello and then, with a vast ransom in hand, returned to his base at Port Royal, Jamaica. Flushed with success he soon continued plundering Spanish targets, first in Cuba and later in what would become Venezuela. For most of this period, Spain and England were not at war, but English authorities continually denied complicity in Morgan's activities and refused to punish him. Morgan continued to ravage Cuba and returned to Panama in 1671 for his most ambitious expedition. Leading what became popularly known as "the great pirate army," he made the first crossing in force of the Isthmus of Panama and sacked Panama City. While an estimated 400,000 pieces of eight were taken, Morgan's men expected more, and in retaliation the city was torched. Upon returning to Jamaica, Morgan learned that England and Spain had already concluded a peace treaty and that his actions were deemed illegal. Spain demanded justice and in 1672 Morgan was arrested as a pirate by the British and taken to London. The next year England was at war with the Dutch, and Morgan's advice on naval affairs was considered good enough to send him back to defend Jamaica—rehabilitated to become deputy governor and a knight of the realm. He died in Jamaica in 1688. (The Diageo rum brand "Captain Morgan" is named for the 17th Century legend.)

## 4. THOMAS TEW

Born into a wealthy Rhode Island family, Thomas Tew's raiding career started in the early 1690s as a legitimate British privateer operating from Bermuda against French ships. Moving to the African coast, he turned pirate, preying on French slavers, and founded a base in Madagascar. From that large island, Tew ranged north into the Red Sea and quickly amassed a fortune. He lived the good life for a few years, returning to the American colonies, but in late 1694 headed back to the Red Sea and West Africa. He died in 1695 in colorful, pirate fashion, holding his guts in his hands after being struck in battle by a cannon ball.

## 5. **WILLIAM KIDD**

Like many pirates, William Kidd's plundering career started as a privateer, attacking the French in the Caribbean. In 1696, in search of a royal commission to enable him to chase greater treasure, he left New York bound for the Red Sea, but soon ran into a problem—the British Navy. Fearful of having much of his crew impressed by the British warships, Kidd rowed away in the night, leaving the Royal Navy to conclude that he must be guilty of something. Now with a reputation as a pirate, Kidd cruised fruitlessly for two years until in 1698 he captured a single large merchantman. But the ship's owner, Muklis Khan, demanded restitution from the East India Company, and Kidd became a wanted man in his native England. Kidd took his prize to the West Indies and finally abandoned the ship on the island of Hispaniola. With his treasure Kidd headed north to New England, and legend has it that he buried his gold on the banks of the Connecticut River. Captured in 1699, Kidd was taken to London and hanged in 1701. And in Connecticut, they're still searching for the gold.

## 6. **EDWARD "BLACKBEARD" TEACH**

Edward Teach earned his fame over a very brief period, turning pirate around 1715 after a career as a privateer against the Spanish. After cruising the Caribbean, Blackbeard based his flagship *Queen Anne's Revenge* in North Carolina, where Teach (or Thatch) shared his booty with the governor. Teach got his nickname from the startling way he tied his long black beard with ribbons and drew the ends over his ears; he was also known to light wicks in his beard during battle. Ultimately, the next-door colony of Virginia grew tired of Blackbeard's piratical actions and dispatched two sloops commanded by Lt. Robert Maynard to run him down. In November 1718, Maynard cornered Teach, and boarding his ship through a ruse, shot him dead and hung Blackbeard's head from his

ship's bow. In 1996 archeologists confirmed that a wreck discovered in Beaufort Inlet, North Carolina, was that of the
*Queen Anne's Revenge.*

### 7. STEDE BONNET

Known as "The Gentleman Pirate," Bonnet had been a plan-
tation owner in Barbados who turned to piracy around 1717.
After taking several prizes, Bonnet's sloop *Revenge* fell in with
Blackbeard, who captured Bonnet and kept him on board
the *Queen Anne's Revenge.* After several months Teach relented, gave Bonnet back his sloop, and let him go. Bonnet,
in turn, was granted a pardon by the governor of North Carolina, acquired letters of marque, and, for a while, chased
Blackbeard. Unsuccessful in that quest, Bonnet returned to
pirating and began calling himself "Captain Thomas." Bonnet
was captured in 1718 and, after escaping prison and being
caught again, was hanged in Charleston, South Carolina.

### 8. TWO GALS AND A GUY

Anne Bonny, Mary Read, and Calico Jack Rackham formed
a highly successful pirating team. While this trio had a fine
time plundering the Caribbean from 1718 to 1720, their rela-
tionships made them more famous than any success in pirating. Anne and Mary were both illegitimate children, Anne from
Ireland and Mary from England. Anne was infatuated with
the pirate life and married a low-level scurvy dog, but soon
took up with Calico Jack Rackham, a fancy who ran a small
pirating operation out of New Providence in the Bahamas.
With Anne at times masquerading as a man, the two led cruises
in the Caribbean, and Anne's loser husband joined the crew.
Anne warmed up to a sailor captured from a Dutch ship who
turned out to be a woman concealing her true identity. This
was Mary, and she and Anne soon let Calico Jack in on their
gender secret and the merriment continued. Mary and Anne

were both more dangerous fighters than Calico, and Jack was no help when the British took the trio and their crew in late 1720. Jack was hanged, Mary died in prison of fever, and Anne escaped death in prison, although the details of her life remain a mystery. She may have been the daughter of a powerful colonial planter, who arranged for her escape from prison and disappearance.

## 9. BARTHOLOMEW "BLACK BART" ROBERTS

By many accounts the most successful pirate of them all was "Black Bart" Roberts, who terrorized the Caribbean beginning around 1720. A fancy dresser—and torturer when it suited him—Roberts got his start in the pirate life when buccaneers captured his ship. When his first captain was killed Bart found himself elected captain and led his new crew in a murderous, pillaging frenzy. Bart cultivated his ruthless reputation, flying a black flag showing himself and Death holding an hourglass. Chased and run down by a British warship off the West African coast, Bart was killed in battle in 1722. His character is the historical basis for Johnny Depp's "Jack Sparrow" in *The Pirates of the Caribbean* movies, although Sparrow is a kinder and gentler version.

## 10. JEAN LAFITTE

One of the most romantic pirate legends belongs to Jean Lafitte, a Frenchman operating out of the Louisiana bayou who threw in with Gen. Andrew Jackson to defend New Orleans against the British attack of January 1815. Although Lafitte commanded only a few dozen men, legend gave him hundreds, even thousands, and grew to stories of him attacking British ships in the Gulf of Mexico. The truth was a bit more prosaic. With his brother Pierre, Jean ran a "Kingdom of Barataria" south of New Orleans and consistently engaged in slave trading (reportedly with Jim Bowie, who later became famous for inventing the Bowie knife and fighting and dying at the Alamo in 1836). His pirate ways did not cease after fighting alongside Jackson, and in 1817 Lafitte was chased from New Orleans to Galveston Island, Texas. Four years later Lafitte again was forced to leave, and his career took a permanent downward turn. Some stories claimed he died of a fever in 1826 but other tales had him living until the early 1850s. Nevertheless, the legend of Lafitte led to numerous films and novels that featured the romantic version of the pirate. A park in Louisiana is named for him, and stories of lost Lafitte treasure still inundate the Gulf Coast.

# Most Famous Admirals

The word *Admiral* is derived from the Arabic *Emir-el-Bahr*, meaning "lord of the sea." The term came into English usage from the French. In 1649, at the time of Oliver Cromwell the Protector of the Kingdom, Army officers were appointed as "Generals at Sea" to command the Navy. During the reign of Charles II (1630–1685) the title was changed to "Admiral" to distinguish Navy leaders from the Army.

The rank of admiral was introduced into the Russian Navy by Peter the Great in 1699; it was discarded from the time of the Russian Revolution in 1917 until 1940. In the U.S. Navy, admiral ranks were introduced in 1862, with David Glasgow Farragut becoming the Navy's first rear admiral.

## 1. THEMISTOCLES (C. 514–C. 449 BCE)

Among his many achievements, the Athenian admiral and statesman played a key role in the victory at the Battle of Salamis, the most important naval encounter of the ancient world. Themistocles fought at the famous Battle of Marathon (492) with little being known about his earlier years, having had humble beginnings. By the time of Marathon he was becoming a leading political-military figure of Athens. He advocated a strong navy to counter threats from Persia. He became a senior commander in the subsequent wars with Persia, and in the decisive Battle of Salamis (480) he commanded the Athenian fleet that inflicted a decisive defeat on the much larger Persian fleet. (He had tricked his fellow Greeks into fighting at Salamis.) Afterwards, his enriching himself through official offices led to his ostracism from Athens circa 474. Themistocles fled to Persia, where he was very well treated.

## 2. VICE-ADMIRAL HORATIO NELSON (1758–1805)

The most famous admiral of the Napoleonic era, Nelson masterminded the British naval victories against the French at the Nile (1798), the Danes at Copenhagen (1801), and the French and Spanish fleets at Trafalgar, off the coast of Spain (1805). Attacking Copenhagen in 1801, when ordered to withdraw, he placed a telescope to his blind eye as a sign that he could not read the senior admiral's signal flags. Nelson was a brilliant tactician; he was admired and respected by fellow officers, loved by ratings, and honored by the British population in spite of his highly publicized, immoral personal life. He died aboard his flagship *Victory* at Trafalgar, having been shot by a French sniper during the savage, close-in encounter with a French warship. Nelson had lost his right eye and right arm in earlier battles. (The *Victory* is preserved at Portsmouth, England, as a memorial.)

## 3. ADMIRAL OF THE NAVY GEORGE DEWEY (1837–1917)

The U.S. Navy admiral who easily defeated the Spanish squadron at Manila Bay in 1898—with the loss of a single American life—Dewey's victory made possible the American occupation of the Philippines. Dewey saw action during the American Civil War and served under Commo. David Farragut. Later, Dewey held the important positions of Chief of the Bureau of Equipment (1889) and President of the Board of Inspection and Survey (1895). Commanding the Asiatic Squadron from 1897, he led his ships against the Spanish fleet in Manila Bay and supported the U.S. Army's capture of the city. Dewey subsequently served as President of the Navy General Board until his death. The six-star rank of Admiral of the Navy was created for him in 1899, although he wore only four stars on his uniform.

### 4. **FLEET ADMIRAL HEIHACHIRO TOGO (1848–1934)**
Togo was the revered Japanese admiral who defeated the Russian Navy in 1904–1905. He took part in the defense against British naval forces in 1863 (age 15) and formally entered the Navy in 1866. Togo served in many sea assignments, including training as a naval cadet in Britain. He fought in several conflicts before commanding the Japanese Fleet against the Russians in 1904–1905, including the devastation of the Russian Fleet at Tsushima in 1905. He then served as Chief of the Navy General Staff and subsequently held honorary posts, being promoted to fleet admiral in 1913. (His flagship from Tsushima, the pre-dreadnought battleship *Mikasa*, is preserved as a memorial.)

### 5. **ADMIRAL OF THE FLEET JOHN JELLICOE (1859–1935)**
Jellicoe commanded Britain's Grand Fleet during the critical Battle of Jutland (1915), when, according to Winston Churchill, "He is the only man who could have lost the war in an afternoon" because of the need to contain the German High Seas Fleet. After a variety of naval assignments, including fighting ashore in China in the Boxer Rebellion, in 1914—at the outbreak of World War I—he became Commander-in-Chief of the Grand Fleet. Although the British were victorious, forcing the German fleet back into port, he was criticized for not inflicting more destruction on the enemy. (In fact, the British lost more ships and men in the battle than did the Germans.)

Jellicoe served as First Sea Lord (1916–1917) and then governor-general of New Zealand.

## 6. ADMIRAL WILLIAM S. SIMS (1858–1936)

An innovative and influential Navy flag officer, Sims commanded U.S. naval forces in Europe during World War I. An advocate of advanced gunnery practices, Sims first saw guns in action as a U.S. observer during the Russo-Japanese conflict of 1904–1905. Promoted to captain in 1911, he became an instructor at the Naval War College and was promoted to rear admiral in 1916. The following year he was named president of the college. He was en route to England with dispatches when the United States entered World War I in April 1917. He was immediately assigned to duty there and became an advocate of the convoy system for defense against U-boats. A month later he became commander of all U.S. naval forces in Europe with the rank of vice admiral. After the war, although having been promoted to full admiral, he reverted to two-star rank and returned to head the Naval War College. After retiring in 1922 he continued to speak and write on naval subjects, advocating air power.

## 7. FLEET ADMIRAL WILLIAM F. ("BULL") HALSEY (1882–1959)

The best-known American admiral of World War II, Halsey was an effective fighting officer and controversial commander. He commanded destroyers early in his career and completed flight training in 1935 (age 52). He was a carrier force commander with his ships approaching Pearl Harbor when the Japanese attacked U.S. naval and air bases in Hawaii on December 7, 1941. Halsey then led the first U.S. carrier strikes against Japanese island bases, and his tenacious leadership helped the United States win the critical Solomons campaign (1942–1943). Although he was not present at the battles of

Adm. William S. Sims was an innovative and influential U.S. naval officer who was an early advocate of advanced gunnery techniques.
*U.S. Navy*

Midway and the Marianas, he led the Third Fleet in its Pacific campaigns. But his fleet's performance during two typhoons and confusion during the battles for Leyte Gulf led to severe controversy. He left active duty in 1947.

## 8. ADMIRAL ISOROKU YAMAMOTO (1884–1943)

As a young officer, Japan's Yamamoto fought and was wounded in the Battle of Tsushima (1905). After a number of assignments, including serving as naval attaché in the United States, Yamamoto served as Commander-in-Chief of the Combined Fleet from 1939. Long an advocate of naval aviation—he held aviation assignments although he was not an aviator—he reorganized the Japanese Fleet to form a strong carrier striking force and conceived the surprise attack on Pearl Harbor; under his plans for six months—as he had predicted—Japan could triumph in the Western Pacific. However, he had no effective plan for a long-term conflict. Yamamoto was killed in a U.S. fighter attack while on an inspection tour in the Solomon Islands.

## 9. GROSSADMIRAL KARL DÖNITZ (1891–1980)

Dönitz commanded the German U-boat force and then the German Navy during World War II, at the end of which he succeeded Adolf Hitler as head of the Third Reich. In World War I he served in a German light cruiser loaned to the Turkish Navy and then commanded a small submarine, which was sunk in October 1918, leading to his capture by the British. Dönitz became an early member of the Nazi Party and admirer of Hitler. In July 1935 he was named commander of the fledgling German submarine force, and in the prewar period he helped build the U-boat force and developed wolf pack tactics. After he directed the U-boat campaign, Hitler made him head of the German Navy on January 30, 1943. Upon Hitler's suicide on April 30, 1945, he became head of the smashed German state—for just over a week. Dönitz was arrested and tried at Nuremberg by the Allies; he served ten years in prison. (Both of his sons died in the war, one in a U-boat and one on a torpedo boat; his daughter's husband also died in a submarine.)

## 10. ADMIRAL OF THE FLEET OF THE SOVIET UNION SERGEI GORSHKOV (1910–1988)

After serving primarily in surface warships, in 1941 Gorshkov was promoted to rear admiral at age 31. During World War II he commanded coastal and river forces in the southern USSR, apparently working briefly with then-political commissar Nikita

Khrushchev. He commanded the Black Sea Fleet in 1951–1955, when he was named Deputy Commander-in-Chief (CinC) of the Navy and became acting head because of illness of the CinC. Formally named CinC of the Navy and a Deputy Minister of Defense in 1956, Gorshkov directed the construction of a highly innovative, world-ranging Soviet fleet. He was retired in 1985 after almost 20 years as CinC.

# Even More Famous Admirals

At least ten additional notable admirals definitely warrant consideration in any "most wanted" listing.

### 1. REAR ADMIRAL JOHN PAUL JONES (1747–1792)
The Scottish-born naval hero of the American Revolution, Jones is cited by some historians as the "father" of the American Navy. When fighting the superior British *Serapis* with his ship *Bonhomme Richard* in 1779, in response to the British commander's demand for his surrender, Jones replied, "I have not yet begun to fight." His highest American rank was commodore. In 1778 he accepted a commission as rear admiral in the Russian Navy and served in the Black Sea until 1789.

### 2. VICE-ADMIRAL WILLIAM BLIGH (1754–1817)
Best known as the commander of the *Bounty*, and then the victim of the mutiny aboard the ship, Bligh was one of the leading ship captains and navigators of his era. He went to sea at age nine and at age 23 joined the famed Captain James Cook's third and final voyage of Pacific exploration in 1776 as master of HMS *Resolution* and overall navigator for the voyage. He sailed for Tahiti in the *Bounty* in 1787 to transplant breadfruit as a food crop for the West Indies. After six

months at the island, when Bligh sailed, several of his men mutinied. Left adrift, he then made an epic, 47-day voyage with 19 of his men in a 23-foot, open boat, sailing 3,600-nautical miles without the loss of a single man. Returning to England, he was acquitted by a court of inquiry and held additional commands, serving with distinction with Nelson at Copenhagen in 1801 in command of HMS *Glatton*.

### 3. **REAR ADMIRAL ALFRED THAYER MAHAN (1840–1914)**

Mahan was the leading naval strategist of his era with his principal work, *The Influence of Sea Power upon History, 1660–1783* (1890), influencing world leaders as well as naval officers. The son of Dennis Hart, a professor at the U.S. Military Academy, he served aboard ship during the American Civil War. Mahan was president of the Naval War College from 1886 to 1889, and commanded one of the new steel cruisers, the USS *Chicago* (later CA 14). He retired in 1896 but was recalled to active service for the Spanish-American War. He was promoted to rear admiral on the retired list in 1906.

### 4. **VICE ADMIRAL STEPAN MAKAROV (1849–1904)**

An innovative Russian naval strategist and tactician, Makarov distinguished himself in the Russo-Turkish War of 1877–1878. He had earlier advocated fast steam-powered ships be armed with torpedoes and proposed the extensive use of mines in naval warfare. His *Discussion of Questions in Naval Tactics* (1897) was a landmark work on naval operations. Makarov was appointed to command the prestigious Baltic Fleet in 1897 and was then sent to the Far East to command the Pacific Squadron in hopes of turning the tide of war against the Japanese. Makarov arrived in February 1904 and after several successful operations, he died when his flagship

*Petropavlovsk* struck a mine on April 13, 1904. His motto was "Remember war!"—every decision should be made as if war were imminent.

### 5. **ADMIRAL OF THE FLEET DAVID BEATTY (1871–1936)**
Born in Ireland, Beatty entered the Royal Navy as a cadet in 1884 at age 13. After service ashore and afloat, including the Boxer Rebellion in China, Beatty commanded several ships before becoming commander of the Battle Cruiser Squadron of the Grand Fleet in 1913. His ships made an important contribution at the Battle of Jutland in 1916 despite the loss of three of his battle cruisers. He was subsequently Commander-in-Chief Grand Fleet (1916–1919) and First Sea Lord (1919–1927). He was known for his good looks and jaunty style.

### 6. **FLEET ADMIRAL ERNEST J. KING (1878–1956)**
The architect of the massive U.S. naval buildup and naval strategy in World War II, King had served in surface ships, submarines, and aviation, earning his pilot's wings in 1927 (at age 48). By the eve of World War II, King's reputation was as an acerbic, intolerant, arrogant lady-killer. His temper was famous for its intemperateness. His stiff-necked attitude seemed to have cost then-Vice Adm. King further promotion, but then, in December 1940, President Franklin D. Roosevelt appointed him commander of U.S. naval forces in the Atlantic and, in late 1941, Commander-in-Chief U.S. Fleet. (King abbreviated the title as *COMINCH*, not the traditional *CINCUS*—he didn't like the latter's sound.) In March 1942, King additionally became Chief of Naval Operations and held the dual posts until his retirement in December 1945. A close friend asked King, "Ernie, how in the world did they ever pick you for the top spot?" King's answer was frank and realistic: "When they get in trouble, they send for us sons-of-bitches."

## 7. FLEET ADMIRAL CHESTER W. nIMITZ (1885–1966)

Nimitz commanded the immense U.S. military effort in the Pacific Ocean areas during World War II. His interests before the war ranged from submarines to refueling ships at sea to carrier tactics. His commands included submarine units, a heavy cruiser, a cruiser division, and a battleship division. When Pearl Harbor was attacked, Rear Adm. Nimitz was Chief of the Bureau of Navigation, which oversaw personnel matters. He was named Commander-in-Chief of the Pacific Fleet and, subsequently, commander of all U.S. military forces in the Pacific Ocean areas. Nimitz devised the strategy for the U.S. westward march toward the Japanese home islands. He was known for his "serene self-control" as well as having a strong grounding in military and naval art. Nimitz prized the intelligence that his codebreaking units derived from interception of Japanese communications, and he used the information often and well. After the war he served two years as Chief of Naval Operations, until December 1947. (His son, Rear Adm. Chester W. Nimitz, Jr., was a submarine commander during the war.)

## 8. REAR ADMIRAL RICHARD E. BYRD (1888–1957)

A leading U.S. Navy aviator and polar explorer, Byrd was credited in 1926 with having been the first man (with his pilot) to have flown over the North Pole. However, subsequent revelations showed that Byrd had flown about 80 percent of the distance to the pole when he was forced to turn back because of an engine oil leak. He began his first of five expeditions to the Antarctic in 1928. Using dog sleds, airplanes, and vehicles, his expeditions—supported in large part by the Navy—mapped much of the frozen continent. His last expedition, a massive undertaking, was in 1955–1956. During World War II he commanded survey missions in the Pacific.

## 9. **ADMIRAL HYMAN GEORGE RICKOVER (1900–1986)**

The controversial "father" of nuclear propulsion, Rickover was born in Russian-controlled Poland. His family brought him to America as a child and he attended the U.S. Naval Academy, after which he entered active naval service in 1922. As a general line officer, Rickover served in destroyers, battleships, and submarines, where he gained a reputation for stoic efficiency. His only ship command was a minesweeper for three months in 1937 in China. During World War II he served with distinction, mostly in the Bureau of Ships where he was in charge of electrical installations in ships. In 1946, Rickover was one of several naval officers and civilians assigned to nuclear propulsion projects (in which the Navy had an interest since 1939). Strongly supported by congressional leaders, Rickover pushed forward the construction of nuclear-propelled surface ships and submarines for the Navy, directing the U.S. Navy's nuclear propulsion program from 1947 until he was "fired" in late 1981.

## 10. **ADMIRAL ARLEIGH A. BURKE (1901–1996)**

The U.S. Navy's most famous destroyer commander, his "Little Beavers" squadron wrought havoc to Japanese forces in the South Pacific in 1943. But Burke was also a leading ordnance expert and intellectual, ending his naval career with an unprecedented six-year tenure as Chief of Naval Operations (1955–1961). As CNO, Burke pushed the Navy into the Polaris missile program and accelerated the adoption of nuclear propulsion for aircraft carriers, surface warships, and submarines. He retired in 1961 after strongly disagreeing with President John F. Kennedy's handling of the aborted Bay of Pigs invasion of Castro's Cuba; reportedly, Kennedy had asked him to serve longer as CNO. His sobriquet was "31-knot Burke," the fighting speed of his destroyers in World War II.

# Admirals Who Died in Combat

In addition to admirals Makarov, Nelson, and Yamamoto, listed previously, the following were among the admirals who died in combat.

### 1. VICE ADMIRAL MAXIMILIAN GRAF VON SPEE (1861–1914)

Von Spee was given command of Germany's East Asia Squadron based at Tsingtao, China, in 1912. From the outbreak of World War I in August 1914, his command concentrated on destroying allied merchant and troop shipping. After a successful engagement with British ships at the Battle of Coronel, off the coast of Chile on November 1, 1914, a far superior British cruiser force surprised his ships in the Falkland Islands. Spee's squadron was decimated on December 8 with the loss of some 2,200 German officers and ratings, including von Spee. (His two sons were also killed in the battle.)

### 2. REAR ADMIRAL ISAAC C. KIDD (1884–1941)

Commander of Battleship Division 1 at Pearl Harbor on December 7, 1941, Kidd rushed to the bridge of his flagship *Arizona* (BB 35) when the Japanese sneak attack began. He was the senior officer afloat in the harbor; as he began giving orders, the *Arizona* exploded, killing Kidd and more than 1,000 sailors and Marines. He was awarded the Medal of Honor for "conspicuous devotion to duty, extraordinary courage, and complete disregard of his own life."

### 3. VICE ADMIRAL MINEICHI KOGA (1885–1944)

The successor to Adm. Yamamoto as Commander-in-Chief of the Combined Fleet, Koga had been commander of Japan's China Area Fleet when World War II began. After several attempts to force the U.S. Pacific Fleet into a decisive battle, on March 31, 1944, he was flying to Davao in the Philippines in anticipation of a major fleet engagement when his aircraft encountered stormy weather and crashed, killing all on board.

### 4. ADMIRAL TOM PHILLIPS (1888–1941)

Phillips commanded the British capital ships *Repulse* and *Prince of Wales* when they were sent to the Far East in 1941 to counter possible Japanese advances into Southeast Asia. On December 10 the two ships were approaching the Japanese landings in Malaya when Japanese land-based bombers attacked them, and both were sunk with heavy casualties, including Phillips.

### 5. VICE ADMIRAL GÜNTHER LÜTJENS (1889–1941)

Lütjens commanded the German battleship *Bismarck* and heavy cruiser *Prinz Eugen* on their sortie into the Atlantic in May 1941 to attack British shipping. At the time the *Bismarck* was Germany's largest warship. After sinking the battle cruiser *Hood*, the German ships were caught and the *Bismarck*, with Lütjens embarked, sunk with heavy loss of life; he was not among the 110 survivors. (The *Prinz Eugen* escaped to a German port in France.)

### 6. **REAR-ADMIRAL KAREL W. F. M. DOORMAN (1889–1942)**

Doorman was commander of the American-British-Dutch-Australian (ABDA) fleet that was engaged by superior Japanese naval forces in the Dutch East Indies in late February 1942. He was lost when his flagship, the heavy cruiser *De Ruyter*, was struck by a Japanese torpedo. He remained in his sinking ship with the wounded who could not be saved.

### 7. **REAR ADMIRAL NORMAN SCOTT (1889–1942)**

An outstanding surface warfare officer, Scott commanded a cruiser on convoy escort duty in the South Pacific at the start of World War II. Subsequently, he commanded a highly effective cruiser-destroyer force fighting in the Solomon Islands. He was killed when his flagship, the light cruiser *Atlanta* (CLAA 51), was fatally damaged by Japanese gunfire and torpedoes off Guadalcanal on November 13, 1942. He was posthumously awarded the Medal of Honor.

### 8. **REAR ADMIRAL DANIEL J. CALLAGHAN (1890–1942)**

Callaghan, a career surface warfare officer, commanded the heavy cruiser *San Francisco* (CA 38) when World War II began. Previously he was the naval aide to President Roosevelt. After participating in early raids against Japanese-held islands, and staff duty, he again went to sea as a crusher-destroyer force commander. He was killed when a 14-inch shell from the Japanese battleship *Kirishima* smashed the bridge of his flagship, the *San Francisco*, on November 13, 1942. He was posthumously awarded the Medal of Honor.

### 9. **VICE ADMIRAL CHUICHI NAGUMO (1887–1944)**

The one-time commander of the First Air Fleet and the carrier force that had swept the seas from Pearl Harbor to Trincomalee in the first months of the war, Vice Adm. Nagumo was largely to blame for the massive Japanese defeat at the Battle of Midway in June 1942. However, Nagumo kept his command of the remaining fast carriers until November 1942. Nagumo was later given the empty command of the Japanese Central Fleet, an entity with its headquarters on Saipan and possessing no major warships. His 6,800 men were among the Japanese forces defeated by the U.S. Marines and soldiers in the June 1944 invasion. He committed suicide in a cave on Saipan on July 6, 1944.

## 10. **VICE ADMIRAL MATOME UGAKI (1890–1945)**

Ugaki had served as chief of staff to Adm. Yamamoto, head of the Japanese Combined Fleet, and, subsequently, commanded major surface forces. As Japan was surrendering on August 15, 1945, Ugaki, then commander of the Fifth Air Fleet on Kyushu, took off with a formation of 11 dive bombers, saying, "I am going to proceed to Okinawa, where our men lost their lives like cherry blossoms, and ram into the arrogant American ships, displaying the real spirit of a Japanese warrior." None of Ugaki's planes reached the American ships off Okinawa; all were lost at sea. Ugaki's posthumously published memoir, *Fading Victory* (1991), is a classic account of the Japanese Navy in World War II.

# Fired or Executed Admirals

### 1. **ADMIRAL OF THE BLUE JOHN BYNG (1704–1757)**

Sent out with a shabby British squadron to reinforce the Mediterranean island of Minorca against a threatened French invasion, he arrived too late and Minorca was lost. For his failure, Adm. Byng was imprisoned, court-martialed, and executed by a firing squad of six marines on the deck of HMS *Monarch*.

### 2. **ADMIRAL FRANÇOIS JOSEPH PAUL DE GRASSE (1722–1788)**

A key player in the American war for independence, Adm. de Grasse served with distinction in several engagements with the British fleet from 1778 to 1781, including the capture of Grenada. In the fall of 1781 he led a French fleet from Saint-Dominique to Hampton Roads, Virginia, where he landed 3,000 French troops to reinforce Gen. George Washington who was facing battle with a British land force. De Grasse then gave battle to a British fleet bringing reinforcements to the area, decisively defeating the British and enabling Washington to force the surrender of Lord Cornwallis, ensuring American victory. Subsequently, de Grasse was defeated in a series of battles against Britain's Adm. Samuel Hood and Adm.

George Rodney. In the latter engagement—the Battle of the Saintes—de Grasse was taken prisoner by the British. His defeats were owing in large part to failures of his captains. Later in 1782 de Grasse was returned to France where he was relieved of all duty, considered a failure by the king, and in 1784 he was court-martialed. Acquitted, he published a memoir, and died in Paris a short time later. DeGrasse was known for his sound grasp of naval tactics and strategy.

### 3. VICE-ADMIRAL ROBERT CALDER (1745–1818)

Calder was second in command of the British fleet prior to Nelson taking command in 1805. That year Calder had chased a larger French and Spanish squadron and, despite an inconclusive battle, was criticized for not having achieved a greater victory. He was relieved of command and court-martialed; he received a severe reprimand for not having done his utmost to renew the engagement, but at the same time he was acquitted of cowardice and disaffection. Nelson said that it was nonsense to expect that any other officer—implying himself—could have done any better. Calder never served at sea again, although he was promoted to full admiral in 1810 because of his seniority.

### 4. ADMIRAL PIERRE CHARLES JEAN BAPTISTE SILVESTRE DE VILLENEUVE (1763–1806)

Villeneuve commanded the French and Spanish fleet that fought at Trafalgar (1805) although he had already been relieved of command by the Emperor Napoleon. The Minister of Marine, en route to Cadiz to replace Villeneuve, was delayed and he sailed. Badly defeated by the British fleet, he was captured and, subsequently, released. He reportedly committed suicide, but the cause of his death remains questionable.

## 5. **ADMIRAL JAMES O. RICHARDSON (1878–1974)**

A distinguished U.S. admiral, Richardson was appointed Commander-in-Chief U.S. Pacific Fleet in January 1940. Concerned about the lack of support facilities at Pearl Harbor, where he had been ordered to base the fleet, he twice went to Washington to appeal the order. He was relieved of his command at President Roosevelt's order and was replaced by Adm. Kimmel in February 1941. (See below.)

## 6. **ADMIRAL HUSBAND E. KIMMEL (1882–1968)**

Kimmel was the U.S. Pacific Fleet commander at Pearl Harbor, Hawaii, when the Japanese attacked on December 7, 1941. He was held largely responsible for the disaster that befell the fleet and was relieved as fleet commander on December 17 (pending the arrival of Adm. Chester W. Nimitz from Washington). Kimmel was not court-martialed but never held another command.

## 7. **VICE ADMIRAL ROBERT L. GHORMLEY (1883–1958)**

Ghormley, commander of U.S. South Pacific Forces from April 1942 to October 1942, was responsible for the highly successful U.S. invasion of Guadalcanal and Tulagi, which began on August 7, 1942. But Adm. Chester W. Nimitz, convinced that Ghormley was "too immersed in detail and not sufficiently bold and aggressive at the right time," replaced him with the more aggressive Vice Adm. William F. Halsey in October 1942.

## 8. **ADMIRAL LOUIS E. DENFELD (1891–1972)**

The U.S. Chief of Naval Operations from December 1947 to November 1949, during the carrier-versus-B-36 bomber controversy of the late 1940s, Denfeld was essentially fired because of his failure to obey the secretary of the Navy with respect to Navy policy statements. He had sought to be renewed as CNO for another two years.

## 9. ADMIRAL OF THE FLEET OF THE SOVIET UNION NIKOLAY KUZNETSOV (1902–1974)

Kuznetsov was fired as Commander-in-Chief of the Soviet Navy—twice! A surface officer, he was appointed to head the Navy by Stalin in 1939 (at age 37) to supervise the building of an ocean-going fleet. Stalin fired and demoted him to rear admiral in 1947, but recalled him to Moscow in 1951 to again supervise the naval buildup. Nikita Khrushchev fired him a second time, in 1956.

## 10. ADMIRAL OF THE FLEET VLADIMIR KUROYEDOV (1944–)

President Vladimir Putin fired Kuroyedov as Commander-in-Chief of the Russian Navy in September 2005. His dismissal came a month after seven Russian sailors became trapped in a midget submarine and had to be rescued with help from Britain. Earlier, the large, nuclear-propelled submarine *Kursk* was lost with the death of 118 Navy men. Indeed, many observers wondered how Kuroyedov had survived the submarine's loss and the botched rescue attempt for several men who survived the initial explosions that sank the submarine. Kuroyedov had been appointed head of the Russian Navy in 1997. Previously, he had served as Chief of the Main Naval Staff and then Deputy CinC of the Pacific Fleet. Kuroyedov had been hospitalized for about two months before his dismissal.

# Aces

The term *Ace* is applied to fighter pilots who have shot down five or more enemy aircraft. The term originated in World War I, but, so far as is known, no naval pilots of any nation accomplished that feat in the 1914–1918 conflict. Fractions of a "kill" were awarded when two or more pilots participated in the destruction of an enemy aircraft. The term *Ace* is also applied to submarine commanders who sink a large number of enemy ships. Unlike the criteria for fighter aces, there are no specific criteria for submarine aces. And while surface ship commanders are rarely considered to be "aces," several certainly rate the accolade in the authors' opinion.

## 1. AMERICAN FIGHTER PILOTS

In World War II some 1,300 American fighter pilots were credited with destroying five or more enemy planes in air-to-air combat. Of those, more than one-third were naval aviators—371 Navy and 124 Marine Corps officers and enlisted pilots. The first Navy fighter ace of the war was Lt.(jg) Edward ("Butch") O'Hare, who, flying an F4F Wildcat from the carrier *Lexington* (CV 2), shot down five Japanese bombers on February 20, 1942; he was credited with a sixth "probable"

43

kill in that engagement. He was shot down during night combat in 1943, having a total record of seven confirmed aerial victories, the last two in the F6F Hellcat.

These American aces made their kills in three fighter aircraft; the leading aces in each aircraft type were:

Grumman F4F/FM Wildcat: Marine Capt. Joseph J. Foss (26+ victories)
Grumman F6F Hellcat: Comdr. David McCampbell (34)
Chance Vought F4U/FG Corsair: Maj. Gregory ("Pappy") Boyington (22 plus 6 in other fighters)

The only naval aviator to score five or more aerial kills in the Korean War (1950–1953) was Navy Lt. Guy P. Bordelon of the carrier *Princeton* (CVA 37), flying from a land base in South Korea. In night operations, piloting an F4U-5N Corsair, he shot down five North Korean piston-engine aircraft in 1953.

The first U.S. fighter aces of the Vietnam War (1962–1972) were Navy Lt. Randy ("Duke") Cunningham and his radar intercept officer Lt.(jg) William ("Irish") Driscoll from the carrier *Constellation* (CVA 64). In 1972, flying an F-4 Phantom, they shot down five North Korean MiG fighters. They were the only Navy fighter aces of that conflict.

## 2. **JAPANESE FIGHTER PILOTS**

The Japanese air forces—Army and Navy—initially did not have a tradition of recording the number of kills by individual pilots. However, as World War II progressed, individual honors for fighter pilots were forthcoming, primarily to improve morale.

The Japanese Navy's first fighter ace was Ens. Kiyoto Koga, who shot down a total of 13 Chinese aircraft in 1937, flying the Mitsubishi A5M Claude fighter. He died the following year after a flying accident.

Comdr. David McCampbell was the top U.S. naval fighter
ace in World War II, downing 34 Japanese aircraft while
flying an F6F Hellcat. *U.S. Navy*

The top-ranking Japanese fighter pilot was Warrant Officer Hiroyoshi Nishizawa with 87 victories, all in the Mitsubishi
A6M Zero. Various figures as high as 150 have been reported
for his aerial victories. He was killed in 1944 when the transport in which he was flying was shot down by U.S. fighters.

### 3. BRITISH FIGHTER PILOTS

The Royal Navy's Fleet Air Arm flew both American- and Brit-
ish-produced aircraft during World War II. The Fleet Air Arm
produced 16 aces during the conflict. The top-scoring fighter
aces in each aircraft type were:

Chance Vought Corsair: Lt. D.J. Sheppard (5 victories)
Fairey Fulmar: Lt. Comdr. S.G. Orr (8.5)
Hawker Sea Hurricane: Lt. Comdr. R.A. Brabner (5)

## 4. GERMAN SUBMARINE ACES

Ship tonnage was measured differently in World Wars I and II. In the earlier conflict, Oberleutnant zur See Reinhold Saltz, who commanded six U-boats in the period 1916–1917, sank 111 merchant ships of 170,500 tons. He died in December 1917 when his submarine, the *UB-81*, struck a mine.

Worthy of special mention is Oberleutnant zur See Otto Weddigen who, in the *U-21*, sank three British armored cruisers off the coast of Holland on September 22, 1914. Firing in succession on the 12,000-ton warships, for the expenditure of five torpedoes he sank all three ships in less than two hours, causing the loss of 1,459 British officers and ratings. Weddigen was lost when the battleship *Dreadnought* rammed the *U-29* in March 1915.

The top scoring German U-boat commander in World War II was Fregattenkapitän Otto Kretschmer. Known as the "tonnage king," he commanded the submarines *U-23* and *U-99*, each for eight war patrols, during which he sank a total of 46 Allied ships of 273,000 tons, including a British destroyer. He was thus the most successful submarine commander of any navy. British warships sank Kretschmer's submarine, and he was captured in 1941.

## 5. BRITISH SUBMARINE ACES

The Royal Navy's top submarine ace of World War II was Lt. Comdr. Malcolm David Wanklyn, commanding the *Upholder*. After service in surface ships, he entered the submarine service in 1933 and in 1940 took command of the *Upholder* while the submarine was under construction. From January 1941 until her loss, for 16 months the *Upholder* was in almost continuous combat in the Mediterranean. The submarine sank or damaged 22 enemy ships of 119,000 tons. These included an enemy submarine and destroyer sunk. Wanklyn, after earning the Victoria Cross, was lost with his entire crew when the *Upholder* was sunk, probably by depth charges from the Italian torpedo boat *Pegaso* off Tripoli in April 1942.

### 6. JAPANESE SUBMARINE ACES

Comdr. Takaichi Kinashi of the Japanese submarine *I-19* is believed to have been Japan's top-scoring submarine commander in World War II. He fired what was probably history's most effective torpedo salvo on September 15, 1942, when the U.S. carrier *Wasp* (CV 7) passed the *I-19* at a distance of only 500 yards. Kinashi fired six Type 95 long-range torpedoes in rapid succession: Three torpedoes struck the carrier, inflicting mortal damage. The three torpedoes that missed the *Wasp* continued traveling toward the carrier *Hornet* (CV 8) task group, the carriers being some 14,000 yards apart when the *Wasp* was struck. One torpedo struck the destroyer *O'Brien* (DD 415), which later sank, and another struck the battleship *North Carolina* (BB 55), inflicting major damage on the ship. After being employed in attacks on Allied shipping, in November 1943 Kinashi sailed the submarine *I-29* across the Indian Ocean, around Africa, and up to a German-held French port. After replenishment and being loaded with war material, the *I-29* was returning to Japan when, on July 26, 1944, the U.S. submarine *Sawfish* (SS 279) torpedoed her in the Luzon Strait. Kinashi and most of the crew of the *I-29* were lost.

### 7. U.S. SUBMARINE ACES

Comdr. Richard H. O'Kane, commanding the submarine *Tang* (SS 306) on five war patrols, sank 24 Japanese ships with a tonnage of 93,824 tons, to become the highest scoring U.S.

submarine skipper. (Wartime estimates credited him with 31 ships of 227,800 tons.) On the night of October 24–25, 1944, the *Tang* was attacking a Japanese convoy near Formosa (Taiwan) when one of her torpedoes made a circular run and struck the submarine, sinking her. O'Kane and seven other survivors were captured by the Japanese. Liberated from Japanese captivity after the war, O'Kane was awarded the Medal of Honor and retired from the Navy in 1957 with the rank of rear admiral.

The U.S. submarine *Flasher* (SS 249) was credited with sinking the most enemy ships by tonnage—21 ships of 100,231 tons—while commanded by Comdrs. George W. Grider and Reuben T. Whitaker.

The most enemy ships were sunk by the submarine *Tautog* (SS 199) under Comdrs. Thomas S. Baskett, William B. Sieglaff, and Joseph H. Willingham. The 26 ships sunk by the *Tautog* totaled 72,606 tons. (O'Kane's *Tang* ranked second with a total of 24 ships and a record ten ships of 39,100 tons for a single war patrol.)

But the highest tonnage for a single war patrol was the submarine *Archerfish* (SS 311), under the command of Lt. Comdr. Joseph F. Enright. Sinking only one ship on her fifth war patrol, early on November 30, 1944, the *Archerfish* torpedoed the Japanese aircraft carrier *Shinano* off Tokyo Bay. She was credited with 59,000 tons for that kill, the *Shinano* being a converted super battleship of the *Yamato* class.

## 8. JOHNNIE WALKER

Capt. F. J. ("Johnnie") Walker was the Royal Navy's most successful anti-submarine group leader. During the war, Walker first commanded the high-scoring 36th Escort Group and then the 2nd Escort Group. The former accounted for 14 U-boats sunk during Walker's tenure, including six destroyed in a 27-day operation in the eastern Atlantic early in 1944.

Walker developed the scheme of "double teaming" a U-boat opponent in his brilliant "creeping" attack tactic: one escort ship slowly kept pace with the submerged submarine by using her echo-ranging Asdic (active sonar). When sufficient data was available for an attack, Walker would have a second escort race in to attack with depth charges. This tactic eliminated the loss of acoustic contact when the attacking escort passed over the U-boat to release depth charges. Walker called this tactic Operation Plaster.

"There were no reports on this tactic to U-boat Command, because once held in the vice of the 2nd [Escort Group]'s Asdic. No U-boat survived. Walker hunted to the death," wrote British historian John Terraine.

Walker died in July 1944—at age 48—of a stroke caused by exhaustion. He had received the Order of Bath and the Distinguished Service Order with three bars for his submarine-hunting exploits.

## 9. **WALTON B. PENDLETON**

Comdr. Walton B. Pendleton commanded the U.S. destroyer escort *England* (DE 635) in May 1944, when she sank six Japanese submarines within a 12-day period. Pendleton, a 1921 graduate of the Naval Academy, had served in battleships and surface warships, and commanded a fleet minesweeper before World War II. In December 1943 he placed the USS *England* in commission and, after workup, took her to the Western Pacific. In May 1944 she was part of a DE group that ran across a picket line of submarines. For his ASW prowess, Pendleton was promoted to commander and received the Navy Cross; the *England* was honored with a Presidential Unit Citation.

Subsequently, on May 9, 1945, the *England* was heavily damaged off Okinawa by a Japanese suicide plane; the attack killed 37 men aboard the ship with many others wounded. She was rebuilt into a high-speed transport. Pendleton retired in 1947 and was promoted to captain on the retired list.

### 10. **DANIEL V. GALLERY**

Commander of a highly effective U.S. anti-submarine group in the Atlantic during World War II, Capt. Daniel V. ("Dan") Gallery's "hunter-killer" group captured a German U-boat, the first enemy warship to be captured by the U.S. Navy on the high seas since the War of 1812.

After service in surface warships, in 1927 Gallery underwent flight training and subsequently served in and commanded aircraft squadrons. In May 1943, as a captain, he was ordered to command the new escort carrier *Guadalcanal* (CVE 60). The "jeep" carrier was the center of an ASW group that included five destroyer escorts. Gallery trained his men hard, and, after their first successes against a U-boat, emphasized techniques for capturing code machines and documents from a damaged submarine that surfaced. His group sank the *U-544* in January 1944, and the *U-68* and *U-515* in April. On the morning of June 4, 1944, the group detected the *U-505* operating submerged some 150 miles off the coast of French West Africa.

Taken by surprise when one of the destroyer escorts depth-charged the U-boat, her captain brought the submarine to the surface and ordered his men to abandon ship. One of the escort ship's crew, well trained under Gallery's guidance, boarded the abandoned submarine. While two sailors raced to the U-boat's radio room to remove cryptographic equipment, other American sailors disconnected the demolition charges the Germans had set and shut off an open waterline. The U-boat was taken in tow by the *Guadalcanal* and brought to Bermuda. The capture contributed greatly to the

Allies' reading of Enigma communications and revealed the secrets of advanced German torpedoes. (The British had previously captured three U-boats at sea.)

At the end of the war, Gallery took command of a fleet carrier. Later, as a rear admiral, he helped direct the U.S. Navy's entrance into the world of guided missiles and nuclear weapons. He retired in late 1960 and wrote nine books and several articles—fact, fancy, and fiction about the Navy.

# Politicians

### 1. THEODORE ROOSEVELT (1858–1919)

The 26th president of the United States, "Teddy" Roosevelt was responsible in large part for the United States becoming a world naval power. An author, explorer, and amateur soldier, he served as Assistant Secretary of the Navy—then the No. 2 post—in 1897–1898. He resigned to form and command the 1st Volunteer Cavalry—the "rough riders"—who fought on foot in Cuba during the Spanish-American War. The epic, high-speed voyage of the U.S. battleship *Oregon* (BB 3) from the U.S. West Coast around South America to join the fleet off Cuba during that conflict led Roosevelt to believe in the importance of a canal across Panama to permit the rapid passage of U.S. warships between the Atlantic and Pacific Oceans. In 1901 he became vice president in the William McKinley administration, and when McKinley was assassinated on September 14, 1901, Roosevelt succeeded to the presidency—the youngest president in American history. He then played an important part in inspiring the Panamanian revolution that ensured future U.S. control of the Panama Canal, with that massive construction project beginning in 1904. Subsequently, Roosevelt developed the idea for an around-the-world cruise by the U.S. battle fleet to demonstrate American sea power. The 16 battleships departed Hampton Roads, Virginia, in December 1907, and undertook a circumnavigation of the world, returning to Hampton Roads in February 1909 (Roosevelt's presidency ended the following month). The battleships and their escorts—painted white—were known as the Great White Fleet. Roosevelt was also the first American to be awarded the Nobel Peace Prize in 1906 for negotiating the peace in the Russo-Japanese War (1904–1905).

## 2. WINSTON CHURCHILL (1874–1965)

A British politician, author, and navalist, Churchill, a graduate of the Sandhurst military academy, saw action with the Malakand Field Force on India's Northwest Frontier, at the Battle of Omdurman in the Sudan, and during the Second Boer War in South Africa. During this period he also gained fame, and considerable notoriety, as a newspaper correspondent. Subsequently, entering politics, Churchill served as First Lord of the Admiralty from 1911. In that post he encouraged the development of naval aviation and was involved with development of the armored tank (which was financed by the Navy), and dispatched Royal Marines to fight in Europe. But his support of the disastrous Dardanelles campaign of 1915 led to his forced resignation from the Admiralty. Remaining a member of Parliament, Churchill served for several months in 1915–1916 on the Western Front as commander of the 6th Battalion of the Royal Scots Fusiliers with the rank of colonel. Between the wars he was a strong advocate of Britain's rearmament in the face of Hitler's buildup of German military forces. With war imminent, Churchill again became First Lord in 1939 and, with the fall of France in May 1940, he became prime minister. Churchill largely conducted the war from his underground Cabinet War Rooms, sitting before a huge map of the world, his military and civilian aides arrayed around him. He traveled extensively to meet with his own military leaders in the field as well as to have talks with Franklin D. Roosevelt, the Soviet Union's Josef Stalin, and China's Chiang Kai-shek. In his communication with Roosevelt, he usually identified himself as a "former naval person." The election of July 1945—with victory over Germany achieved—saw a Labour election and Churchill was turned out of office. He again served as prime minister in 1951–1955. Churchill was the most literate of any national leader of the period and had a technical understanding of military strategy and tactics—a circumstance that, combined with an apparently inexhaustible energy, plagued British military leaders throughout World War II. He won the Nobel Prize in Literature in 1953 for his historical writings.

### 3. FRANKLIN D. ROOSEVELT (1882–1945)

The 32nd president of the United States, Roosevelt was responsible for the buildup of the U.S. Navy between the world wars and for the direction of American strategy in World War II. He was a fifth cousin to President Theodore Roosevelt, whom he greatly admired. Franklin Roosevelt served as Assistant Secretary of the Navy—still the No. 2 job in the Navy—from 1913 to 1920. He entered the White House in 1933 and, with the nation in a deep economic depression, he used shipbuilding as a tool to help economic recovery. In 1935, Roosevelt pushed the first Neutrality Act through Congress to help keep America out of European conflicts. Renewed several times, the act permitted Roosevelt to use U.S. naval air and surface forces to help the British track German submarines in the Atlantic after World War II began in Europe in September 1939. In secret meetings in Washington with British leader Winston Churchill and the Anglo-American military staffs, Roosevelt helped develop a strategy of defeating Germany first and then Japan when the United States entered the war. With the

Japanese attack on the United States on December 7, 1941, Roosevelt—working closely with Churchill—developed the master strategy for the Allied victory. In April 1945, Roosevelt died of a cerebral hemorrhage—three weeks before Germany's surrender.

### 4. JOHN F. KENNEDY (1917–1963)

The 35th president of the United States, Kennedy was the first U.S. president to have served in the Navy. Kennedy tried to enlist in the Army in 1941, but was rejected because of his chronic back trouble. Through family connections he was accepted into the Navy three months before the Japanese attack on Pearl Harbor. He was assigned to PT boat duty and in the spring of 1943, as a lieutenant (junior grade), he took command of *PT 109* at Tulagi, an island in the Solomon Islands. U.S. PT boats patrolled "The Slot" (Georgia Sound) that ran between two groups of islands. Japanese convoys were using The Slot as a passage for reinforcing their garrisons in the Solomons. During the summer of 1943, Kennedy's PT boat and several others were ordered to intercept Japanese warships and transports attempting to reinforce Japanese-held islands. On the night of August 2–3, Kennedy's PT boat was lying in wait to attack Japanese ships transiting The Slot. One of the Japanese destroyers, barreling up The Slot, rammed the *PT 109*. Two American sailors were killed instantly. Kennedy rescued at least one of the badly injured men. The survivors clung to the hulk of the PT boat through the night, then he led them to a little atoll they named Bird Island. Through cooperative native islanders, the survivors got word to an Australian coastwatcher who arranged for their rescue. The Kennedy saga, well publicized in newspapers and then in a *New Yorker* magazine article by John Hersey, became part of the Kennedy legend. But, once, when someone remarked on his heroism, Kennedy is reported to have said, "It was involuntary. They sank my boat." Kennedy remained in the Navy until January 1945, then entered politics, was elected to the House of Representatives from Massachusetts in 1946 and to the Senate in 1952. He served as president from January 1961 until his assassination on November 22, 1963. Kennedy's senior honors essay at Harvard on England's appeasement policy was published in 1940 as *Why England Slept*, a title riposte to Winston Churchill's *While England Slept* (1938).

## 5. LYNDON B. JOHNSON (1908–1973)
The 36th president of the United States, Johnson succeeded to the presidency upon the assassination of John F. Kennedy in November 1963. A member of Congress since 1937,

John F. Kennedy sits in the cockpit of his motor torpedo boat *PT 109*. *U.S. Navy*

Johnson was a lieutenant commander in the Naval Reserve. In 1941 he told his constituents that if a war started he "would be in the front line, in the trenches, in the mud and blood with your boys, helping to do that fighting." Soon after the Pearl Harbor attack he entered active service in the Navy and was sent to the West Coast on an inspection tour of shipyards and war production plants. President Roosevelt then sent Johnson on an inspection tour of the Southwest Pacific. He flew as a passenger on a B-26 Marauder bomber attacking a Japanese air base on New Guinea, which was attacked by Japanese fighters. After the mission he was awarded a Silver Star by Gen. Douglas MacArthur. On July 8, 1942, President Roosevelt ordered all congressmen in the armed forces to return to Washington. Johnson served as president from November 1963 to January 1969.

### 6. RICHARD M. NIXON (1913–1994)

The 37th president of the United States, Nixon served during World War II as a Navy lieutenant, initially assigned to the Naval Air Transport Service. Nixon, a California lawyer, had gone to Washington to work for the Office of Price Administration. As a lawyer he received a direct commission as a lieutenant (junior grade). After training, he was sent to New Caledonia, a South Pacific island that served as a landing site for U.S. aircraft being ferried to Australia. In October 1945 he left active duty and entered the Naval Reserve. He was a commander in the reserve in 1953 when he took office as vice president to General of the Army Dwight D. Eisenhower. Nixon served as president from January 1969 until his resignation in August 1974.

### 7. GERALD R. FORD (1913–2006)

The 38th president of the United States, Ford served briefly as a naval officer in World War II. He succeeded to the presidency in August 1974 upon the resignation of President Nixon. Ford, as assistant navigation officer and director of physical education aboard the light carrier *Monterey* (CVL 26) during the war, saw action in the Pacific. Lt.Comdr. Ford was discharged in 1946 and resumed his war-interrupted legal career, and entered politics. He served as president through January 1977.

### 8. JIMMY CARTER (1924–)

The 39th president of the United States, Carter was the first chief executive who had graduated from the U.S. Naval Academy. He had a brief Navy career, mainly in submarines. After the academy (Class of 1946) he served in surface ships and in a diesel-electric submarine. He was selected for nuclear power training, and had orders to the Navy's second nuclear-propelled submarine, the USS *Seawolf* (SSN 575), when his father died in 1953. Carter immediately resigned his commission to handle family affairs. He became president in January 1977, and shortly afterwards went aboard a nuclear-propelled submarine for the first time, the USS *Los Angeles* (SSN 688). He served as president until January 1981.

### 9. GEORGE H. W. BUSH (1924–)

The 41st president of the United States, Bush flew a carrier-based torpedo bomber in World War II and was shot down while on a bombing mission. He was reputed to be the youngest pilot in the U.S. Navy during the war. He was assigned to a TBM Avenger torpedo squadron flying from the USS *San Jacinto* (CVL 30) in 1944, and saw significant action in the Pacific. On September 2, 1944, his plane was hit by anti-aircraft fire over Japan's Bonin Islands near Okinawa. He and his two crewmen bailed out after the plane was damaged. The crewmen were lost. Bush was in the water for about an hour, at times being under fire from Japanese shore guns, until the U.S. submarine *Finback* (SS 230) rescued him. Bush was awarded the Distinguished Flying Cross for the mission. After the war he attended Yale University and entered the oil business and politics. He served in Congress and as head of the Central Intelligence Agency, becoming president in January 1989; he served one term. His son George W. Bush was the 43rd president of the United States.

## 10. JOHN S. MCCAIN III (1936–)

McCain was the first career naval officer to be a serious presidential candidate. His father and grandfather were both four-star admirals. A Naval Academy graduate (Class of 1958), McCain became a naval aviator and flew A-4 Skyhawk attack planes in the Vietnam War. He was aboard the carrier *Forrestal* (CVA 59) in 1967 when the ship was devastated by a fire that began on the flight deck near McCain's aircraft. He volunteered to continue flying attack aircraft from another carrier and was on his 23rd combat mission when his plane was shot down over North Vietnam. Badly injured, he was captured and spent five and a half years in prison, enduring extreme torture and privation. When his captors realized that he was the son of the admiral commanding U.S. forces in the Pacific, he was offered immediate release from prison, but refused. McCain served on active duty until 1981, retiring as captain. He entered politics and served in the House and the Senate, and was a candidate for the Republican presidential nomination in 2000. He was the Republican candidate for president in 2008.

# Oldest Preserved Warships

For centuries there were few clear differences between ships built specifically for combat and armed merchant ships, and determining what qualifies as an old warship rather than simply an old ship is open to interpretation. The oldest ships are likely those unearthed from ancient Egyptian, Chinese, and Imperial Roman times, or the remains of the "Jesus boat," a craft found on Lake Galilee that dates back some 2,000 years. Most were likely built for ceremonial or commercial purposes. A number of war craft from the Middle Ages have been unearthed in Northern Europe, and several well-preserved Viking ships are on display in Scandinavian countries.

The ships listed here were clearly built by countries for naval purposes. Ships for which only significant parts are on display—such as several ships from the American Civil War, including the turret from the American Civil War *Monitor*—are not included.

(The Historic Naval Ships Association at http://www.hnsa.org maintains an excellent list of preserved warships online.)

## 1. *MARY ROSE* (LAUNCHED C. 1509)

One of the largest ships in England in the early 16th Century was the *Mary Rose*, built between 1509 and 1511. She was part of a fleet assembled by King Henry VIII to meet a threatening French fleet. Fully loaded for battle, the warship ponderously sailed on July 19, 1545, to meet the foe just outside Portsmouth, England, but a gust of wind heeled her gunports too close to the water, and, in view of the monarch, the ship rolled over and sank. Sucked into the bottom's muck, the *Mary Rose* was preserved by mud for more than 400 years until she was discovered in the 1960s. The wreck was raised in 1982 and it is preserved inside a special dock at the Portsmouth Dockyard, along with thousands of artifacts recovered from the wreck.

## 2. *VASA* (LAUNCHED 1627)

Put to sea in Stockholm harbor on a sunny August 10, 1628, the mighty *Vasa*'s festive maiden voyage quickly turned to tragedy when she heeled in the wind, rapidly took on water, and sank, carrying several dozen people to their deaths. She lay on the bottom of the harbor until 1961 when the wreck, well preserved after 333 years in the Baltic's cold, fresh waters, was raised and brought to shore. The ship now is the centerpiece of a major museum complex in Stockholm.

## 3. *VICTORY* (LAUNCHED 1765)

Officially described as "the world's oldest surviving warship still in use," HMS *Victory* is the last representative of the "wooden walls of England" that defended the empire for several centuries. The ship achieved fame as the flagship of Lord Horatio Nelson during the Battle of Trafalgar in 1805, where Nelson died while leading his fleet to victory over a combined French and Spanish fleet. The *Victory* left frontline service in 1812 to become a fixture in the harbor of England's great naval base at Portsmouth. The ship-of-the-line was permanently moved into drydock in 1922, later tilled with concrete, and remains a major tourist attraction at the Portsmouth Dockyard, steps from the preserved ships *Mary Rose* and *Warrior*.

### 4. *PHILADELPHIA* (LAUNCHED 1776)

This small gunboat is the oldest preserved warship in North America, a veteran of the American War of Independence. Part of a fleet built in 1776 on Lake Champlain by Benedict Arnold (before he switched sides to the British), the *Philadelphia* was scuttled in 1776. She was raised in 1935 and now is on display at the Smithsonian Institution in Washington, D.C.

### 5. *CONSTITUTION* (LAUNCHED 1797)

The sailing frigate *Constitution* remains an afloat, fully commissioned warship of the U.S. Navy, with an active-duty commanding officer and crew. Recognized in 2004 by Guinness World Records as the world's oldest commissioned warship afloat, the frigate is berthed at the former Charleston Navy Yard in Boston, Massachusetts, near where she was built. She is maintained in a near-operational condition following a rebuilding in the 1990s that included fabrication of new sails. The frigate leaves her berth several times a year for cruises in Boston Harbor.

### 6. *CONSTELLATION* (LAUNCHED 1854)

The builders of this sailing sloop used materials from the famous frigate *Constellation* of 1797, a move that caused decades of confusion and argument over the surviving ship's true origin. She was one of the last large sailing warships built for the U.S. Navy and is the last naval Civil War-era vessel still afloat. The sloop survived as a training ship until her retirement by the Navy in 1955, when a preservation group acquired her and brought her to Baltimore, Maryland. After

The USS *Constitution*, completed in 1798, is the world's oldest warship still in commission and afloat. *U.S. Navy*

several decades of fitful ownership and chronic deterioration, a major restoration project completed in 1999 has restored the ship to her former glory.

### 7. *WARRIOR* (LAUNCHED 1860)

Despite her status as Britain's first iron-hulled, steam-powered warship, the frigate *Warrior* owes her remarkable survival to being long used after her active service as a lowly fuel hulk in Wales. Acquired by a preservation trust in 1979, the stripped and dismasted hulk was the focus of a major restoration project and emerged in 1987 magnificently transformed to her original state. The frigate now is afloat at the

Portsmouth Dockyard in England, footsteps from HMS *Victory* and the *Mary Rose*.

### 8. *HUASCAR* (LAUNCHED 1865)
This iron-hull, turreted ram was first part of a secret plan by the Confederate States to build modern warships in Europe during the American Civil War. The Union government discovered the plans and forced most of the countries involved in the shipbuilding to cancel the sales. The *Huascar*, built in Britain, instead was sold to Peru and fought against Chile in the War of the Pacific. The Chileans captured her in battle in 1879 and commissioned her into the Chilean Navy. Chile has maintained the ship in an excellent condition as a tribute to the battle, and the ship is preserved today at Talcahuano. Peru still insists that the ship should be returned.

### 9. *BUFFEL* (LAUNCHED 1867) AND *SCHORPIOEN* (LAUNCHED 1868)
The ironclad ram *Schorpioen* was built in France and sold to the Netherlands, where she served for four decades before conversion to an accommodations ship. The hulk survived the World War II occupation by Germany and was acquired in 1982 by a preservation group, which restored the ship and opened her to the public in 1989 at the naval base in Den Helder. The *Buffel* is another ironclad ram that was to become a Confederate ship; she was built in Scotland and sold on completion to the Netherlands, where, like the similar *Schorpioen*, she survived as an accommodations hulk. The ship was bought by the city of Rotterdam in 1974 and restored to her original appearance.

### 10. *OLYMPIA* (LAUNCHED 1892)
The protected cruiser *Olympia* (C 6) is the oldest steel-hulled American warship still afloat and owes her survival to the fame

acquired as the flagship of Commo. George Dewey at his 1898 victory over a Spanish fleet at the Battle of Manila Bay. The Navy kept the ship as a relic until 1957, when she was trans-ferred to a Philadelphia, Pennsylvania, group, and today is on exhibit in the City of Brotherly Love, the last surviving naval combatant of the Spanish-American War.

# Battleships

The battleship—or dreadnought, or battlewagon—remains the most romantic of naval warships, even though the ponderous ships rarely fought each other. In the 1980s the United States briefly returned the four battleships of the *Iowa* (BB 61) class to active service, giving new generations the chance to see the big-gun ships for real. Now, all have been permanently retired and turned into museums, but their ability to stir imaginations lives on.

### 1. THE FIRST

The term "battleship" evolved over time from the line-of-battle sailing ship, while the turreted ship grew from early coast-defense monitors. There was no "first battleship" as such. The American Civil War-era *Monitor* was the world's first warship with a gun turret, but the British *Devastation*, launched in 1871, was perhaps the first ship combining true "battleship" qualities: The steel ship, displacing 9,188 tons, mounted four 12-inch muzzle-loading guns in twin turrets plus smaller caliber guns. By the early 20th Century, however, the idea of a ship carrying a large number of a single size of big gun produced the ultimate battleship form, named for the first ship to be completed to the idea—the British *Dreadnought* of 1906, the "all big-gun battleship." That ship mounted ten 12-inch guns in twin turrets and had steam turbines providing the unprecedented speed of 21 knots. While nearly all subsequent battleships could be called dreadnoughts, the Italians actually thought of the idea first, and the Americans designed and began building the *South Carolina* (BB 26) class before the British ship, which was built faster. The U.S. ships were capable of almost 19 knots and carried eight 12-inch guns. All subsequent battleships followed their pattern.

## 2. LARGEST EVER BUILT

The Japanese sister ships *Yamato* and *Musashi* were by far the largest battleships that ever put to sea, but just how big they were remains unclear, as sources disagree. They displaced at least 65,000 tons full load—about 7,000 tons more than the American battleships of the *Iowa* (BB 61) class—and some reputable sources list 72,000 tons. Their nine 18.1-inch guns were the largest ever to go to sea. But they never fired their guns in anger at opposing dreadnoughts and both were sunk late in World War II by U.S. carrier-based aircraft. A third sister ship, the *Shinano*, was completed as an aircraft carrier—and was quickly sunk by the U.S. submarine *Archerfish* (SS 311).

## 3. LARGEST EVER PLANNED

The American battleships of the *Montana* (BB 67) class would have displaced 58,000 tons standard and about 70,500 tons full load had they been built. They were cancelled in 1943, none having been laid down. By that time the U.S. Navy's leadership realized that the battleships and battle cruisers already built and under construction would be sufficient for fighting the Japanese and that shipbuilding efforts and materials could be put to better use in constructing aircraft carriers and landing ships. Other very large battleships that advanced either into the serious planning or early construction stages were the Soviet *Sovyetskiy Soyuz* class of about 65,000 tons, which were never built because of the German invasion of the USSR, and the German *H*-class battleships at 62,500 tons, cancelled early in World War II.

## 4. FASTEST

Unquestionably the fastest battleships ever built were the four American ships of the *Iowa* (BB 61) class. Just how fast they ever moved in service, however, is not so clearly documented. The ships were designed for 32.5 knots, and all attained or exceeded that speed on trials in 1943–1944. The *New Jersey* (BB 62) reportedly reached 35.2 knots during machinery trials for her 1968 reactivation. The three others ships are also reported to have reached 35 knots in service. That remarkable speed for ships with a 45,000-ton standard displacement was accomplished with four steam turbines (eight boilers) generating 212,000 shaft horsepower. Their range was also impressive: 5,300 nautical miles at 29.6 knots, 15,900 nautical miles at 17 knots, and 18,000 nautical miles at 12 knots.

## 5. THE MOST TURRETS

This is a superlative for which there is only one contender: HMS *Agincourt*, the only battleship ever built with seven main-battery turrets—each named for a day of the week. Originally ordered by Brazil to be built in Britain, the ship represented South American dreams of grandeur and carried one more turret than the six-turret American *Wyoming* (BB 32) and Japanese *Fuso* classes. Taken over by the Royal Navy during World War I, the *Agincourt*'s excessive number of turrets, with twin 12-inch guns, however, strained the hull and stretched damage control requirements, and was never repeated.

Construction of the ship—the only one of her design—as the *Rio de Janeiro* was begun in 1911, but Brazil realized the ship was too expensive and sold her early in 1914 to Turkey, which assigned the name *Sultan Osman I*. When World War I erupted in August of that year Britain requisitioned most of the warships then under construction for foreign powers in the United Kingdom, including the Turkish battleship. That move, combined with Germany's offer of a battle cruiser to Turkey, which happened to be in the Mediterranean at the time, contributed heavily to Turkey's decision to enter the war on Germany's side.

## 6. MOST GUNS

The Japanese super battleships *Yamato* and *Musashi* mounted more guns than any other warships. In addition to their main battery of unprecedented size—nine 18.1-inch guns—the ships mounted a secondary (anti-ship) battery of six 6.1-inch (155-mm) guns. In addition to the above guns, the ships had massive anti-aircraft batteries:

|                        | Yamato | Musashi |
| ---------------------- | ------ | ------- |
| 5-inch (127-mm) twin   | 24     | 12      |
| 1-inch (25-mm) triple  | 138    | 156     |
| .50-cal (13-mm) triple | 6      | 6       |
| Total guns             | 183    | 189     |

The U.S. battleships of the *Iowa* (BB 61) class mounted an impressive nominal armament of 157 guns: nine 16-inch guns, 20 5-inch dual-purpose guns, 80 40-mm Bofors anti-aircraft guns, and up to 80 20-mm Oerlikon anti-aircraft guns. The U.S. battleships' anti-air capabilities were far superior to those of the Japanese ships—both sunk by carrier-based air attack—because of superior radar and fire control directors, and the use of proximity-fuzed ammunition for the 5-inch guns.

## 7. **MOST FAMOUS**

There is no doubt that the 1941 breakout of the German *Bismarck,* accompanied by the heavy cruiser *Prinz Eugen*, is one of the most famous sea chases of all time. The tale is recounted in numerous books and the very good 1960 movie *Sink the Bismarck*, and was revived by a 2001 expedition to the ship's wreck. But the American *Arizona* (BB 39) wins this category, simply because the dramatic explosion of the dreadnought during the December 7, 1941, Japanese attack on Pearl Harbor is recounted by the U.S. Navy, public, and media every December 7. She remains on the bottom of Pearl Harbor, where about one and a half million visitors board the ship's memorial each year.

## 8. **MOST REMEMBERED On FILM**

Few viewers realize it, but millions of people have watched the sinkings of Austria-Hungary's *Szent Istvan* and Britain's *Barham* on film—although in nearly every case, the scenes are used as stand-ins for other ill-fated battleships. Now relatively obscure, these are the only battleships at sea ever to have their sinkings filmed. The sinking of the *Arizona* (BB 39) also was captured on film, but that ship was tied up in harbor. The Austro-Hungarian battleship was torpedoed and sunk in June 1918 by an Italian motor torpedo boat, and the last half hour of the ship's life was filmed from a sister ship; 89 sailors died when the ship rolled over and sank. The loss of the *Barham* on November 25, 1941, sunk by three torpedoes from the German *U-331*, was far more tragic, as 861 sailors were killed when the ship's magazines exploded as she capsized. A great many television and cinema productions use this footage (including a number of instances where they're used to depict the sinking of the *Arizona*), including many instances where scenes of both ships are cut together to represent one event.

## 9. LAST TO BE BUILT

Only two nations completed battleships after the end of World War II: Great Britain and France. Early in 1939 the British Admiralty decided to build a single new battleship that would use the 15-inch gun turrets originally fitted in the battle cruisers *Courageous* and *Glorious*, which had been converted to aircraft carriers. Having the guns available would speed construction of the new dreadnought. Named *Vanguard*, the 46,000-ton warship was completed in August 1946 with a main armament of eight 15-inch guns. She was decommissioned in 1959 and scrapped.

Construction of France's *Jean Bart* began in 1936, and the incomplete ship escaped to Morocco in June 1940 as the Germans overran most of France. Although tied up in Casablanca, the partially armed ship was damaged in a long-range gunnery duel with the American battleship *Massachusetts* (BB 59) during the Allied invasion of November 1942. While the battleship was widely recognized as obsolescent by 1945, post-war public opinion in France heavily favored completing the ship for prestige reasons, and construction resumed in the late 1940s, albeit at a slow rate. It was not until May 1955 that the ship was fully commissioned, but she remained in service for only some six years and was decommissioned in 1961 and scrapped. The *Jean Bart* displaced 48,950 tons standard and was armed with eight 15-inch guns in the unusual arrangement of two quad turrets forward.

## 10. LAST TO SERVE

Following the Korean War (1950–1953), the U.S. Navy kept the four battleships of the *Iowa* (BB 61) class in reserve in the event that the nine 16-inch guns on each ship would be needed for shore bombardment. The *New Jersey* (BB 62) was briefly activated in 1968 during the Vietnam War but quickly decommissioned as too expensive, and few ever expected the ships to see any more service. But the Reagan-era military buildup begun in 1981 saw the ships as valuable assets, and all four were reconditioned, partially modernized, and put back into service between 1984 and 1988. The collapse of the Soviet Union, however, resulted in a major drawdown of U.S. military forces and the four *Iowas* were again mothballed. Last to serve was the *Missouri* (BB 63), which hauled down her commission pennant on March 31, 1992. (That ship had been the scene of the Japanese surrender ceremony in Tokyo Bay on September 2, 1945.) Politics and "battleship groupies" played a role in keeping the ships a few more years in various stages of reserve, but the last two in Navy custody, the *Iowa* and *Wisconsin* (BB 64), were stricken in March 2006.

# Cruisers

There is no beginning and no end in sight for this most eclectic class of warships. Ranging in size from giant battle cruisers to small scouting ships, cruisers have been built to take on the widest variety of missions and roles. As this volume went to press, the U.S. Navy was planning a new cruiser class—designated CG(X). Some member of Congress even advocated nuclear propulsion for the ships.

## 1. LARGEST

The 42,100-ton British battle cruiser *Hood*, armed with nine 16-inch guns and having a speed of 32 knots, reigned between the World Wars as the world's largest and fastest warship—one of the most impressive ships ever built following her completion in 1920. The battle cruiser was the upper extreme of the wide diversity of types developed as cruisers. But she sacrificed a battleship's armor for her speed, and hence was an easy mark for the German battleship *Bismarck* and heavy cruiser *Prinz Eugen* in their brief fight on May 24, 1941. The *Hood* sank with the loss of 1,338 of her crew; there were three survivors.

## 2. **FASTEST**

Always a topic of dispute, as cruisers—particularly those of
Italy and France in the period between the world wars—were
often built to reach widely publicized trials speeds, some in
excess of 40 knots, that were never attainable in operational
service. The U.S. anti-aircraft cruisers of the *Atlanta* (CLAA
51) class of the early 1940s are often reported as being the
fastest ever built, but those stories also seem to have been
hyperbole. Those 6,000-ton ships—armed with 16 5-inch
dual-purpose guns—were officially rated at 31.6 knots, but
undoubtedly reached 33 knots, as did most other U.S. war-
built cruisers.

## 3. **LARGEST CLASS**

The 27 light cruisers completed as the U.S. *Cleveland* (CL 55)
class built during World War II would have belonged to an
even larger class had the Navy not decided to convert nine
others into aircraft carriers and to cancel the construction of
three more. These 10,000-ton ships were armed with 12 6-
inch guns as well as a heavy dual-purpose and anti-aircraft
armament.

## 4. **FIRST MISSILE CRUISER**

The U.S. Navy in the early 1950s converted the heavy cruisers *Boston* (CA 69) and *Canberra* (CA 70), completed as 8-
inch gun cruisers in 1943, into the world's first ships armed
with guided missiles (redesignated CAG 1 and CAG 2,
respectively). After their triple 8-inch gun turret and other
structure were removed, they each were fitted with two twin
launchers for the Terrier surface-to-air missile. The ships
retained their two forward 8-inch triple turrets.

## 5. **FIRST NUCLEAR CRUISER**

The USS *Long Beach* (CGN 9), completed in 1961, was the world's first nuclear-propelled cruiser and first nuclear surface warship. She was predated by the USS *Nautilus* (SSN 571), completed in 1955, as the first nuclear warship, and by the Soviet icebreaker *Lenin* (1959) as the first nuclear surface ship. The 14,200-ton, 721-foot *Long Beach* was completed without any guns, being armed with two twin Terrier and a twin Talos launcher for surface-to-air missiles. Space and weight were provided for installation of Regulus surface-to-surface cruise missiles and, subsequently, Polaris ballistic missiles, but those weapons were never installed. The U.S. Navy built eight additional cruiser-type ships with nuclear propulsion, all much smaller than the *Long Beach,* while the Soviet Union built four larger nuclear cruisers of the *Kirov* class.

## 6. **LAST GUN CRUISER IN SERVICE**

Two all-gun heavy cruisers lasted in service into the mid-1970s: the Spanish *Canarias* and the U.S. *Newport News* (CA 148). Both ships were decommissioned in 1975, and Spain struck the *Canarias* from its ship list in December 1975 and put her up for sale. The United States held on to the *Newport News* for a few years more, and struck the ship in 1978—the year that Spain scrapped the *Canarias*. The *Newport News* was scrapped in 1994. Her sister ship *Des Moines* (CA 134), in mothballs since 1961, was scrapped in 2007, while a third sister ship, the *Salem* (CA 139), is preserved at Quincy, Massachusetts. Britain's last gun cruiser, HMS *Belfast,* is preserved at London, while the British light cruiser *Caroline*, a veteran of the Battle of Jutland in 1916, remains in existence as a reserve training ship at Belfast, Northern Ireland. The three Salem-class ships, completed in 1948–1949, were the largest "heavy" cruisers (8-inch guns) built by any nation, displacing 16,000 tons standard.

## 7. MOST ILL-CONCEIVED

The battle cruiser—of which HMS *Hood* was the largest ever built—was a sexy, exciting, and romantic idea that also was a death trap for thousands of sailors. The idea was to build a ship as big as a battleship—even bigger in some cases—with battleship-size big guns, but armored on a lesser scale to permit greater speed. When matched up with each other the results could be spectacularly deadly: three British battle cruisers blew up in action on May 31, 1916, at the Battle of Jutland, prompting the British battle cruiser commander, Vice-Adm. David Beatty, to mutter, "there seems to be something wrong with our bloody ships today." The British, who developed the type, built the most true battle cruisers. Of 13 ships completed, five were sunk in battle, all with very high casualties. (See Largest American, below.)

## 8. LARGEST AMERICAN

The largest American cruisers to enter service were the two large cruisers of the *Alaska* (CB 1) class, informally but almost invariably referred to as battle cruisers. However, unlike their often ill-fated predecessors, the *Alaska* and her sister ship *Guam* (CB 2) were "balanced" with respect to armor, speed, and weapons. Completed in 1944, they served in the Pacific late in World War II. The *Alaska*s displaced 27,500 tons standard, mounted nine 12-inch guns, and were capable of 33 knots. Their service careers were brief. Three sister ships were never completed; one, the *Hawaii* (CB 3), was held onto for several years with various plans put forth to complete her as a fleet command ship (CBC) or missile cruiser (CBG).

In World War I the United States began construction of six large battle cruisers of the *Lexington* (CC 1) class. They were to have been 43,500-ton ships mounting eight 16-inch guns with a 33.25-knot speed. In the event, two were converted during construction to large aircraft carriers, the *Lexington* (CV 2) and *Saratoga* (CV 3); the others were scrapped on the building ways.

### 9. MOST SUCCESSFUL

The 3,650-ton German light cruiser *Emden* perhaps gave the most bang for the buck of any warship. In a World War I combat career that lasted *just over three months*, the diminutive warship captured or sank 23 merchant ships totaling 101,182 tons, sank a Russian light cruiser and a French destroyer, led dozens of British and Japanese warships on a chase across the eastern Indian Ocean, and caused the diversion of merchant shipping throughout the region. She was finally caught and sunk by the much larger Australian cruiser *Sydney* on November 9, 1914, but the German ship's exploits and gallantry of her commander, Karl von Müller, garnered worldwide attention and admiration. The *Emden*, completed in 1909, was armed with ten 4.1-inch guns.

### 10. LARGEST GUNS

The British "large light cruiser" *Furious* of World War I was intended to mount two 18-inch guns in single-gun turrets forward and aft, but was completed with only one monster gun, mounted aft. The forward end of the ship was converted for flying operations, and the ship eventually was fully converted to an aircraft carrier. It was the largest gun ever fitted to a British warship, and only the Japanese battleships *Yamato* and *Musashi*, each with nine 18.1-inch weapons, had larger guns.

# Destroyers

The destroyer-type warship evolved from the need for a ship to counter the dozens of small torpedo boats that emerged in the late 19th Century. Larger, faster, and more heavily armed than the torpedo boats, the torpedo boat destroyer eventually replaced the smaller ship in most of the world's navies. In the 20th Century the destroyer evolved into an anti-submarine ship and torpedo carrier intended to attack enemy fleets, then into a jack-of-all trades.

## 1. FIRST DESTROYER

The world's first torpedo boat destroyer was the 348-ton Spanish *Destructor*, launched in 1886. But the ship was too slow and not considered successful in its intended role. The first true torpedo boat destroyers were ordered in Britain in 1893 and became HMS *Havoc* and *Hornet*. The first American destroyer was the USS *Bainbridge* (DD 1), which joined the fleet in 1900.

## 2. FIRST SUNK IN ACTION

The Spanish destroyers *Furor* and *Pluton* were part of a Spanish squadron trapped in Cuba in 1898 during the Spanish-American War. They were sunk, along with most of their squadron, by U.S. warships on July 3, 1898.

### 3. FASTEST

As with cruisers, it's impossible to tell which destroyers could accurately claim the title of fastest ever built, as many ships attained artificially high speeds on trials before entering ser-vice—speeds that the ships rarely if ever attained during their operational lives. The French *Le Terrible*-class destroyers of the 1930s possibly hold the speed title, as they routinely topped 40 knots in service.

### 4. LARGEST

While some claim the ships do not properly belong in the destroyer category, the U.S. Navy's new 14,000-ton *Zumwalt* (DDG 1000) class now under construction will be—by a wide margin—the largest destroyer type ships ever built. The first of the 14,000-ton ships is expected to enter service in 2013. The ships will be armed with two 155-mm Advanced Gun Systems (AGS) as well as surface-to-air and land-attack missiles.

### 5. BIGGEST GUNS

While the German Navy armed a number of destroyers in World Wars I and II with 5.9-inch guns, the U.S. destroyer *Hull* (DD 945) was experimentally fitted in 1975 with an au-tomatic 8-inch Major Caliber Lightweight Gun (MCLWG). The experiment was judged a success, but the weapon was re-moved in 1979 and that gun program was cancelled. Ships of the *Zumwalt* (DDG 1000) class will each carry two 155-mm automatic weapons that will be, except for the *Hull*'s 8-inch gun, the largest-caliber weapons to be fitted to a destroyer.

### 6. FIRST MISSILE SHIP

The USS *Gyatt* (DD 712) became the world's first destroyer armed with guided missiles when converted in 1955 to a guided missile ship (DDG 1) with a twin Terrier surface-to-air missile launcher aft. Later U.S. destroyers were armed with the smaller Tartar missile launcher. The *Gyatt* was built during World War II as a 2,400-ton ship of the *Gearing* (DD 710) class orginally armed with six 5-inch guns and ten 21-inch torpedo tubes.

### 7. **FIRST GAS TURBINE**

Although several ships were fitted experimentally with gas turbines—including the British destroyer *Matapan*—the Soviet Kashin class of "large anti-submarine ships" became the world's first operational gas turbine warships when they entered service in the early 1960s. These were fast, 38-knot, graceful ships armed with four 3-inch guns, five torpedo tubes, and two surface-to-air twin missile launchers. Several of the 20 ships of this class were later fitted with Styx short-range surface-to-surface missiles. Six modified Kashins were built in the Soviet Union for the Indian Navy.

### 8. **LARGEST CLASS**

The 175 ships of the U.S. *Fletcher* (DD-445) class, built from 1941 to 1945, were the most numerous class of destroyer ever built by any navy. Although the last active ship of the class was withdrawn from the U.S. Navy in 1971, dozens more sailed on in foreign navies, with Taiwan decommissioning its final three ships of the class in 1999. At least one more ship remained in service longer (see below). The *Fletchers* displaced 2,050 tons standard, and carried a heavy armament of five 5-inch guns and ten 21-inch torpedo tubes, plus light guns and anti-submarine weapons. They could make 35 knots in service.

## 9. LAST GUN DESTROYER

The last non-guided-missile destroyer in the U.S. Navy was the USS *Cushing* (DD 985) of the *Spruance* (DD 951) class, which was decommissioned on September 21, 2005. All remaining destroyers in the U.S. Navy are missile-armed ships designated DDG. However, while the *Cushing* lacked surface-to-air missiles that provide the DDG designation, the *Cushing* and all other *Spruance*-class destroyers could carry Tomahawk land-attack cruise missiles.

## 10. LONGEST-SERVING DESTROYER

The ex-USS *John Rodgers* (DD 574) of the U.S. *Fletcher* class is probably the longest-serving destroyer in history. Commissioned in 1943, she was transferred in 1970 to Mexico as the *Cuitlahuac*. The ship remained in service until at least July 2001 (and perhaps another year, as sources differ)—a career of at least 58 years.

# Frigates and Modern Escorts

The term *frigate* has evolved perhaps as much as any ship type if not more. In Nelson's day it meant a fast yet powerful sailing ship, but the classification fell out of favor with the advent of steel and iron hulls, and steam propulsion. The term was revived by the British early in World War II to refer to a ship smaller than a destroyer but larger than a corvette, intended largely for the anti-submarine role and derived from the Royal Navy's pre-war sloops. The U.S. Navy's counterpart destroyer escorts (DE) were begun as Lend-Lease ships for Britain. Soon after World War II the U.S. Navy began building a series of ships larger than destroyers and called them frigates (designated DL; with guided missiles, DLG; and, with nuclear propulsion, DLGN). Most of the post-war U.S. frigates approached small cruisers in size; indeed, the first of these ships, the USS *Norfolk* was actually begun as a cruiser (CLK 1, changed to DL 1). By the 1970s the situation had become most confusing, and in 1975 the U.S. Navy relented, reclassifying its frigates as destroyers or cruisers and calling its destroyer escorts—by then known as ocean escorts—frigates. Modern frigates can be quite large and powerful warships, while the corvette is a smaller ship. In modern use there are no clear lines of demarcation across international navies between what is a destroyer, frigate, or corvette—essentially it's all a matter of degree.

### 1. MODERN FRIGATES: THE *BITTERN* CLASS

British frigates evolved from sloops—a type which officially was dropped from the lexicon in 1937 when all such ships were recast as escorts. What would become the classic World War II anti-submarine ship was derived from the *Bittern* class of 1933. These were 1,600-ton ships intended to handle a variety of patrol and escort missions. Their armament varied, but the *Bittern* was completed with three 4-inch twin anti-aircraft mounts—a major capability in the years before the war. By 1938 the *Black Swan* class was under construction. Of similar size to the *Bittern*, the *Black Swans* were capable ships that gave excellent war service, but they were too complex and expensive for wartime mass production.

### 2. CORVETTES: THE FLOWER CLASS

After the Munich crisis of 1938 the British Admiralty drew up plans to get the fleet on a war footing within two years. One of the urgent needs was for great numbers of escort ships, and something was needed that could be built simply and quickly by dozens of small shipyards unaccustomed to naval work. William Reed of Smith's Dock Company in northeast England proposed a vessel based on that company's whaling ship *Southern Pride*. From that humble beginning arose a building program in Britain and Canada that produced 135 ships over the next four years. The basic design was for a 940-ton ship with an overall length of 205 feet, crewed by 47 men (with that number soon being increased). The tiny ships formed the bulk of early North Atlantic convoy escorts and performed heroically in appalling weather conditions, holding the line until more sophisticated ships could be built. And,

19 of these ships, generally armed with a single 4-inch gun, lighter weapons, and lots of depth charges, that were built in Canada were provided to the U.S. Navy in 1942–1943 under "reverse Lend-Lease" to help fight U-boats.

### 3. LIGHT DESTROYERS: THE HUNT CLASS

The idea of a "light destroyer" that would be cheaper than the fleet type was appealing to several navies in the 1920s and 1930s. In the fall of 1938 the British began development of a small warship that could handle a variety of escort and other duties normally performed by fleet destroyers. The new ship would not quite have the speed of its big brothers—so they could not screen the battle fleet—and would be less expensive. The result was the Hunt class, a remarkably handy warship of 900 tons, 280 feet long, armed with two 4-inch twin anti-aircraft gun mounts and capable of 26 knots. (Later ships in the class were slightly larger with most mounting six 4-inch guns.) When the ships first entered service in 1940 they lacked the range needed for an ocean convoy escort, but proved quite adept at close quarters combat in the waters of the North Sea and the English Channel. A total of 86 ships in four variants were built through 1942, and the idea sparked development across the Atlantic as well.

### 4. THE AMERICAN DESTROYER ESCORTS

For about two years, beginning in 1939, the U.S. Navy debated the wisdom of building a small destroyer. While cheaper than a bigger ship, many senior officers felt that the cost savings weren't worth the loss of speed, range, and fighting power. The issue was finally settled in August 1941 when the British asked if the Americans could build 100 escort destroyers and President Franklin Roosevelt approved the Lend-Lease production of the first 50 British destroyer escorts, or BDEs. Construction of the first ships was begun at the Navy Yard in

Boston, the cradle of the American Revolution against British rule. The first BDE was HMS *Bayntun*. But after America's entry into the war in December 1941, the need for U.S. escorts grew exponentially, and a number of the BDEs were completed for the U.S. Navy, which ordered hundreds of the ships for itself. The first U.S. Navy DE was the USS *Evarts* (DE 5), which was begun as one of the British Lend-Lease ships and completed in 1943. The *Evarts* displaced 1,436 tons and was 289½ feet long, with an armament of three 3-inch dual-purpose guns—and lots of depth charges. Later DE types were 306 feet long and displaced about the same tonnage. These had the same 3-inch gun battery or, in later ships, two 5-inch dual-purpose guns, and all had three 21-inch torpedo tubes for use against surface ships or a U-boat caught in a close-in fight. A total of 1,005 wartime DEs were planned for the British and U.S. Navies, although just over 550 were completed during and just after the war—still an impressive number considering all the other warships and merchant ships being constructed in U.S. yards. Many DEs were converted into high-speed transports (APD) or, after the war, radar picket ships (DER).

### 5. CANADA'S CORVETTE COMMANDS

The overwhelming bulk of Canada's naval contribution to World War II was in the dozens of small corvettes and frigates that fought the fierce winter weather of the North Atlantic and Canadian Maritimes to protect the vital convoys keeping Britain alive and a base for the assault on Nazi-dominated Europe. The creation of this force was one of Canada's greatest efforts: There were no war-built escorts in service at the beginning of 1940, but two years later 96 Flower-class corvettes and Bangor-class minesweeper escorts were in service. By the beginning of 1944, 87 Flowers, 16 River-class frigates, 53 Bangors, 5 Algerine-class sloops, and 7 Isles-class trawlers were in commission—no less than 168 ships. Eventually the maple-leafed Flower corvettes became a prime symbol of Canada's war effort, and one, the *Sackville*, is preserved today at Halifax, Nova Scotia. This contribution to the naval war in the North Atlantic allowed Canada to develop a larger fleet after the war, including an aircraft carrier, modern destroyers, and submarines. The Royal Canadian Air Force joined in the anti-submarine effort, and, flying American-built Catalinas and Liberators, made a significant contribution to the air side of the effort.

## 6. DESTROYER ESCORTS CAPTURE A U-BOAT

The German submarine *U-505* was a hard-luck boat. In 1943 her commanding officer committed suicide during a depth charge attack—the only time in the war such an event took place—but the boat survived. On her next patrol the submarine suffered an even more humiliating fate and became the only German submarine captured in combat during World War II by the U.S. Navy. Capt. Daniel V. Gallery, in command of a hunter-killer group that consisted of an escort or "jeep" carrier and escorting ships, had noticed that German submariners were becoming sloppy when abandoning ship after being attacked and were failing to set explosives to blow their ships up. Gambling that this would be the case, he laid out plans for his destroyer escorts to try to capture a submarine. Sure enough, on June 4, 1944, his group forced a U-boat to the surface off the west coast of Africa. The crew abandoned ship and, with the submarine filling with water and underway with a jammed rudder, a brave group of sailors from the destroyer escort *Pillsbury* (DE 133) led by Lt.(jg) Albert David, clambered aboard the submarine. Working in darkness, not knowing if the ship was ready to blow up, the men disconnected the demolition charges and stopped the flooding. For the first time since the 19th Century American sailors had captured an enemy warship on the high seas. Sworn to secrecy, the men of the escort group could celebrate only amongst themselves, but after the war the U-boat found its way to Chicago, Gallery's home town, and today is preserved there as a museum. The *U-505* was a treasure trove of U-boat secrets, including several advanced acoustic homing torpedoes.

## 7. THE ACES OF ACES

The U.S. destroyer escort *England* (DE 635) holds the record for the individual ship sinking the most enemy submarines—six. In May 1944, in anticipation of a U.S. Navy-Marine thrust into the Western Pacific, the Japanese Navy stationed 13 submarines in a line to give early warning of the American advance. U.S. codebreakers learned of the Japanese action and dispatched an anti-submarine group to the patrol line. On May 19, 1944, one of the group, the *England,* attacked and sank the submarine *I-16.* Over a 12-day period—despite the group commander allowing other DEs to "shoot first"—the *England*, under Comdr. Walton B. Pendleton, sank six Japanese subs. Later, on May 9, 1945, the *England* was struck by a Japanese suicide plane and severely damaged. She was rebuilt as a high-speed transport (APD) and continued to serve in the Navy. After learning of her anti-submarine exploits, the Commander-in-Chief U.S. Fleet, Adm. Ernest J. King, said that "there will always be an *England* in the U.S. Navy." But no ship in the U.S. Navy now carries that name. (The DE *England* was named for a Navy ensign killed at Pearl Harbor on December 7, 1941.)

## 8. THE MODERN POST-WAR FRIGATE

The need for a capable, ocean-going anti-submarine ship able to chase Soviet submarines continued to grew during the Cold War. A number of World War II-era destroyers were converted to escort roles and several small escort classes were developed, but none were truly satisfactory. For the U.S. Navy, the break came with the *Bronstein* class of the early 1960s. Large, 372-foot-long ocean escorts of 2,723 tons, they were the smallest ships capable of carrying the large SQS-26 sonar, the most powerful U.S. sonar at the time. The new ships carried ASROC (Anti-Submarine Rocket) and 3-inch guns. Later classes carried 5-inch guns and within a few years a new, missile-armed type, the DEG ("G" for guided missile) was developed. Even more important, helicopters—first DASH radio-controlled drones and then manned helicopters—gave the ships a long-range delivery system for anti-submarine torpedoes and nuclear depth bombs. By the end of the Cold War the U.S. Navy had more than one hundred of these ships in service to escort amphibious ships and convoys and form anti-submarine groups. In 1975, when the "frigate" term was belatedly applied to these ships—that term was used by most of the world's navies for such ships—they were all reclassified as FF or, with guided missiles, FFG.

## 9. THE ULTIMATE CORVETTE?

The small, fast, and lethal warship has been a goal for generations. Some think that Swedish designers have come close to the ideal with the *Visby*-class corvettes. The 236-foot-long ships displace about 700 tons and are built of carbon-fiber composite materials to save weight. Able to top 35 knots, they take ship stealth characteristics to a new level, and are functionally invisible—they actually carry radar reflectors to mount when in heavily trafficked areas. The first ship went to sea in 2005 and Sweden has so far built a total of five. Budget restrictions have eliminated several features that would have been installed on the ships, including anti-missile weapons, but they may be restored in the future. The ships are armed with a rapid-fire 57-mm cannon and anti-submarine weapons, and can embark a small helicopter.

## 10. **THE LITTORAL COMBAT SHIP**

From the 1970s on, modern frigates have grown into true multi-purpose warships and are, in many navies, essentially destroyers. Many are as large as 5,000 or 6,000 tons. In the United States the most recent trend has been for something smaller and—hopefully—less expensive. The result is the littoral combat ship, or LCS, a ship of about 2,800 tons that takes the concept of modularity farther than ever in a warship design. The idea is for a high-speed warship (about 45 knots) that will take on extra equipment, sensors, and weapons in a package known as a "mission module" to carry out specialized assignments: initially anti-submarine, anti-surface, and anti-mine warfare. Fitted with large flight decks and hangars, and a mission bay area to handle the modules, the ships are to fight in contested waters like the Persian Gulf or the Yellow Sea. In 2004 two designs were chosen to compete with each other, and the Navy plans to test the ships against each other to select the design for series production: Lockheed Martin's *Freedom* (LCS 1) and, from General Dynamics, the *Independence* (LCS 2). A total of 55 ships are planned, but stay tuned for further developments as the lead ships of both designs have far, far exceeded their initial cost estimates.

# Aircraft Carriers

## 1. FIRST AIRCRAFT CARRIER

The world's first aircraft carrier, that is, built or converted specifically to operate wheeled aircraft, was HMS *Furious*. Converted during construction from a light battle cruiser, the *Furious* was completed in 1917 with a flying-off deck forward (above a hangar) and an 18-inch gun aft. She subsequently underwent numerous modifications and conversions, serving as a first-line aircraft carrier until the end of World War II.

Two ships vie for the honor of being the world's first built-for-the-purpose aircraft carrier: The British *Hermes* was the world's first ship begun as an aircraft carrier, work on her having started in January 1918; she was launched on September 11, 1919, but with the urgency of war past she was not completed until July 1923. The Japanese *Hosho* (Flying Phoenix) was laid down on December 19, 1919, and completed in December 1922.

## 2. FIRST ESCORT CARRIER

The world's first escort carrier was HMS *Audacity*, converted in 1940–1941 from the captured German merchant ship *Hanover*. As a carrier the ship had no elevators or hangar deck and her eight Martlet fighters (F4F Wildcats) were maintained on the flight deck. The *Audacity*—after highly successful operations as a convoy escort—was sunk on December 21, 1941, torpedoed by the German *U-751*.

### 3. FIRST NUCLEAR CARRIER

The USS *Enterprise* (CVAN 65), completed in 1961, was the world's first nuclear-propelled aircraft carrier. (After the USS *Long Beach* [CGN 9], completed earlier that year, she was the world's second nuclear surface warship.) At the time the "Big E" was the world's largest warship. Only the subsequent nuclear carriers of the *Nimitz* (CVN 68) class are larger.

### 4. FIRST SHORE BOMBARDMENT

What is believed to have been the first and the only shore bombardment by an aircraft carrier occurred during the Korean War when, on September 22, 1951, the British maintenance carrier *Unicorn* closed with the coast just north of the 38th Parallel and used her 4-inch guns to bombard North Korean positions. That was a unique activity for aircraft carriers.

### 5. FIRST SUPER CARRIER

The first so-called "super carrier" was to have been the *United States* (CVA 58), laid down at Newport News, Virginia, on April 18, 1949; she was cancelled five days later. The ship was to have had a standard displacement of almost 67,000 tons and be 83,200 tons full load.

The first super carrier to be completed was the USS *Forrestal* (CVA 59), placed in commission on October 1, 1955. The ship served in the Cold War and participated in the Vietnam War, being taken out of service in 1993.

## 6. FIRST CARRIER SUNK IN COMBAT

HMS *Courageous* was the first aircraft carrier to be sunk, being torpedoed by the German *U-29* on September 17, 1939, two weeks after the start of World War II. At the time the carrier was engaged in anti-submarine operations with four destroyers. Struck by two torpedoes, the *Courageous* sank in 15 minutes, taking with her 519 of her crew of 1,260 officers and ratings.

## 7. FIRST CARRIER SUNK BY GUNFIRE

The first and only large aircraft carrier to be sunk by gunfire was HMS *Glorious* on June 8, 1940, by the German battle cruisers *Gneisenau* and *Scharnhorst*. The carrier, steaming from Norway to Britain, with no aircraft ready for takeoff, was sunk by salvos of 11-inch shells, with her two escorting destroyers also being sunk. In the battles for Leyte Gulf in October 1944, the U.S. escort carrier *Gambier Bay* (CVE 73) was sunk by Japanese gunfire, and the Japanese light carrier *Chitose* was sunk by a combination of U.S. aircraft and surface ships.

## 8. FIRST CARRIER SUNK BY AIRCRAFT

The British carrier *Hermes* was sunk in the Indian Ocean near Ceylon on April 9, 1942. Attacked by a Japanese carrier-launched force of 63 dive bombers escorted by nine fighters, 20 minutes after the first bomb struck the *Hermes* she was on the bottom of the Indian Ocean, ripped apart by at least 20 direct hits. The number of direct hits may have been as high as 40, with the deluge of bombs making it impossible for either the Japanese fliers or British survivors to accurately count them. The Japanese planes also sank the destroyer accompanying the carrier.

## 9. LARGEST CARRIER OF WORLD WAR II

The largest aircraft carrier built in World War II was the Japanese *Shinano*, converted during construction from a *Yamato*-class super battleship. Completed in November 1944 and not yet operational, the *Shinano* was sunk on the 29th of that month by the U.S. submarine *Archerfish* (SS 311). The *Shinano* displaced 62,000 tons standard and was to displace 73,040 tons full load.

## 10. LARGEST CARRIER EVER BUILT

The largest warships ever constructed are the ten nuclear-propelled aircraft carriers of the *Nimitz* (CVN 68) class. The lead ship, commissioned on May 3, 1975, had a standard displacement of 81,600 tons and a full load displacement of 91,400 tons. As subsequent ships were built each was slightly modified, leading to an increase in full load displacement until the final ship of the class, the *George H.W. Bush* (CVN 77), completed in 2008, has a full load displacement in excess of 100,000 tons with a length of 1,100 feet.

The USS *Nimitz* (CVN 68) was the lead ship of a class of ten aircraft carriers that are the largest warships ever built. *U.S. Navy*

# Raiders

Raider warfare always has been the naval strategy of the weaker force. Faced with overwhelming odds, a handful of ships from a weak navy can force a stronger opponent to send dozens of warships to cover vast areas as they search for the lone wolf. The most successful raider campaigns were carried out by the Confederates in the American Civil War and the Germans in both world wars. Radar, improved radio communications, and aircraft eventually put an end to one of the most romantic of all forms of warfare.

## 1. *ALABAMA*

This most famous of all Confederate raiders was built for that purpose in England. Under a false identity she slipped past a Union frigate to make her getaway from Liverpool during the summer of 1862 and then, under Capt. Raphael Semmes, began nearly two years of raider warfare. From the North Atlantic to the Caribbean, thence to the Indian Ocean and the East Indies, the *Alabama* took more than 60 prizes and sank the Union warship *Hatteras* off Galveston, Texas. In June 1864 Semmes was finally cornered by the Union steam sloop *Kearsarge* in Cherbourg, France. Accepting the Union offer of a duel, the raider was sunk by superior gunnery as thousands watched from the French shore, but Semmes was saved by a British yacht and escaped. After the war Britain agreed to pay an indemnity of $15.5 million to the U.S. government as reparations for losses inflicted by the raiders *Alabama, Florida,* and *Shenandoah.*

### 2. *FLORIDA*

Also built in England with Confederate money, the twin-stack *Florida*'s career lasted only a few months longer than that of the *Alabama.* She began her raiding cruise by running the Union blockade into Mobile, Alabama, then made her escape to take a total of 33 prizes. Cornered by Union ships in Halifax, Nova Scotia, she slipped away at night via a little-used dangerous and narrow channel. Fate caught up with her when the Union steam sloop *Wachusett,* in violation of international law, attacked the Confederate "illegally" at anchor in the harbor of Bahia, Brazil, on October 7, 1864, then towed her to sea as a prize.

### 3. *SHENANDOAH*

The *Shenandoah* was purchased new in England in the fall of 1864 and was destined to become the last Confederate raider, carrying on with the war for many months after the Civil War officially ended. After raising the Stars and Bars off Portugal, she took six prizes in the South Atlantic before heading to Australia. Then, in the spring of 1865, she began a devastating campaign in the Northern Pacific against the Union whaling fleets. Not until August 1865 did the ship learn of Lee's surrender in April from newspapers aboard captured whalers, and the *Shenandoah* headed back to England where she surrendered in November.

## 4. *EMDEN*

When World War I broke out in August 1914, the German cruiser squadron based in China realized its situation was untenable and began a long cruise across the Pacific in an ill-fated attempt to reach home. One ship, the small cruiser *Emden*, was detached to conduct raider warfare in the squadron's wake and draw off potential pursuers. Under Capt. Karl von Müller, the little ship succeeded beyond all expectations. Cruising through the Dutch East Indies, the Bay of Bengal, and the Indian Ocean, Müller captured or sank 21 merchant ships, destroyed two warships, shelled Penang and Madras, disrupted shipping schedules, and tied down dozens of powerful pursuing Allied warships, all the while earning worldwide fame for the gallant conduct of his crew. After three months of creating havoc, the Germans were cornered and destroyed by the much larger Australian cruiser *Sydney* in the Cocos Islands, but a small group of Germans managed to escape aboard a leaky wooden schooner.

## 5. *SEEADLER*

Although not the highest-scoring German raider of World War I, the *Seeadler* gained fame by being the only one with a full suit of sails, and was the last square-rigged sailing ship used as a warship. Under Count Felix von Luckner, the raider left Germany in late 1916 and sank 14 Allied merchant vessels in the Atlantic and Pacific oceans—11 of them sailing ships. Although the *Seeadler*'s career ended when she was wrecked by a tidal wave in the Society Islands, the colorful von Luckner became a highly sought lecturer after the war, touring the United States with his friend and biographer Lowell Thomas throughout the 1920s.

## 6. *WOLF*

Unlike most German raiders of World War I, the *Wolf* shook up the Allies by laying minefields in areas where they were least expected. During a 445-day cruise from late 1916 into 1918, the raider laid mines off the Cape of Good Hope and Karachi, India, and outfitted a captured British prize as a mine-layer. Although up to 55 warships at a time were searching for the German, she eluded her hunters to return to Germany, having sunk 15 ships with mines and captured or sunk 12 more.

## 7. *ADMIRAL GRAF SPEE*

Conventional warships usually made less than satisfactory merchant raiders, but for the first three months of World War II the German "pocket battleship" *Admiral Graf Spee* turned in a good effort. Under Capt. Hans Langsdorff she sank nine merchant ships and tied up just as many British warship-hunting groups crisscrossing the South Atlantic and Indian Oceans. Langsdorff played by the rules and no lives were lost in any of the sinkings. The ship's luck ran out on the morning of December 14, 1939, when three British cruisers—the *Exeter, Ajax,* and *Achilles*—found the German raider in the South Atlantic. Rather than avoid battle, as standard engagement rules dictated, Langsdorff instead chose to fight it out with his adversaries. In the ensuing Battle of the River Plate the Germans nearly sank the *Exeter* and damaged the other two cruisers, but suffered damage themselves. Langsdorff then made a serious tactical error and entered the neutral port of Montevideo, Uruguay. After three days of international intrigue played out in the worldwide media, the ship headed to sea and blew herself up rather than face defeat by a reinforced British squadron. Afterwards Langsdorff, who never espoused the Nazi Party line, committed suicide.

## 8. *ATLANTIS*

Perhaps the most successful of all German raiders, the end of the *Atlantis* was helped along by the timely publishing of photographs of the ship in the weekly *Life* magazine. For 602 days, from March 1940 until November 1941, Capt. Bernhard Rogge's ship ranged across the South Atlantic and Indian Oceans, sinking 22 merchant ships of 144,000 tons. A *Life* magazine photographer was aboard one of the prizes in April 1941 and managed to smuggle some of the photos he shot back to New York, where they were published in the June 23, 1941, issue of *Life*. The images gave British authorities their first conclusive look at the mysterious raider, which was subsequently caught and sunk in the South Atlantic by the British heavy cruiser *Devonshire*.

## 9. *PINGUIN*

Another raider that cruised at the same time as the *Atlantis* was the *Pinguin*. Living up to her name she cruised to Antarctica and terrorized the Norwegian whaling fleet, capturing three factory ships and 11 whalers. All told, in a cruise lasting 320 days, she sank or captured 32 ships of 155,000 tons. The total included four ships sunk by mines laid by the raider or one of her prizes. Like her sister ship *Atlantis*, the *Pinguin* was sunk by a British heavy cruiser, in this case HMS *Cornwall*. Capt. Ernst Felix Krüder went down with his ship, along with 341 Germans and 214 of his prisoners.

## 10. *KORMORAN*

With a final tally of 12 ships of 75,000 tons, the 351-day cruise of the *Kormoran* was not the most successful raider effort of World War II. But it certainly ended in the most spectacular fashion: in battle with the Australian light cruiser *Sydney*—which was sunk with all hands. The ships met on November

19, 1941—a week after the *Atlantis* was sunk—off the coast of Western Australia. The *Sydney* challenged the raider, which was in disguise, and approached to less than a mile from the suspected ship. Then the *Kormoran* dropped her disguise and opened fire, scoring quick hits and starting major fires. The *Sydney* replied with 6-inch gunfire and delivered fatal blows to the raider, which sank as the Australians drifted over the horizon, burning fiercely. More than 300 Germans survived the raider's sinking, but the *Sydney* and her entire 645-man crew were never seen again.

# Spy Ships and Spyplanes

The Cold War was in large part an intelligence conflict, with both the Western alliance and the Soviet Union and its allies seeking out secrets of the other side. The following are the more significant and interesting naval aspects of the conflict.

### 1. PB4Y-2 PRIVATEER

The U.S. Navy adopted the famed B-24 Liberator four-engine, long-range bomber as a maritime patrol aircraft late in World War II. The navalized version was the PB4Y-2 Privateer, which first flew in 1943 and was easily distinguished from the twin-tail Liberator by its single, tall tail fin. The naval aircraft was heavily armed and configured for long-endurance, low-level flights carrying a heavy bomb load. After the war several Privateers were fitted for electronic reconnaissance and flew surveillance missions along the Soviet periphery. One of these "ferrets" became the first shootdown of a Western spyplane by the Soviets on April 8, 1950. That Privateer, flying from Wiesbaden, West Germany, was shot down by piston engine fighters off the coast of Latvia. All ten Americans on board were killed.

## 2. AGI SPY SHIPS

The U.S.-NATO designation for Soviet spy ships during the Cold War was AGI. Beginning in the 1950s, the Soviet Union initially employed modified trawler-type AGIs to collect intelligence in overseas areas and to observe Western naval operations. Although often depicted in the Western press as "disguised" fishing trawlers, the Soviet intelligence collection ships were readily identifiable: All were Navy manned and fitted with extensive electronic antennas, and some were armed. Later AGIs were built on trawler hulls because their large, insulated cargo holds were readily adaptable to electronic equipment bays and crew berthing spaces. Trawler hulls also provided long endurance, had good seakeeping qualities, and were in series production. The large ships of the *Primor'ye* class (3,700 tons, 278 feet) and *Bal'zam* class (5,400 tons, 346 feet) were capable of on-board intelligence processing as well as collection, thus accelerating the delivery of intelligence data to fleet and regional commanders. By the late 1990s—just before the demise of the Soviet regime—some 60 AGIs were being operated by the Soviet Navy.

## 3. BEAR-D

The Soviet "Bear"—which first flew in 1952—is one of history's most-versatile and long-lived combat aircraft. Its accolades include being one of the fastest propeller-driven aircraft in history and the only swept-wing turboprop aircraft of any nation to achieve first-line status as a combat aircraft. And, by any criteria, it must be considered one of the most attractive aircraft to take to the skies. The Tupolev Tu-20/Tu-95 bombers series included the naval Bear-D reconnaissance variant fitted with a massive ventral surface search radar. These naval Bears sought out Western warships and targeted them for missile attacks; they did not carry bombs or missiles. Some Bear-D aircraft flew from bases on the Kola Peninsula, around

Norway's North Cape, and south to land in Cuba without stopping or refueling in flight.

### 4. USS *LIBERTY*

The U.S. Navy spy ship *Liberty* (AGTR 5) was steaming in the Mediterranean off the Sinai coast on June 8, 1967, during the Arab-Israeli Six-Day War when she was attacked by Israeli aircraft and torpedo boats. The *Liberty* was a converted merchant ship, packed with electronic intercept equipment and specialized technicians. She was sent into the area to monitor communications of Soviet forces that were supporting the Arab states. In a series of command and reconnaissance foulups, the Israelis mistook the *Liberty* for an Egyptian ship. The attacks left the ship heavily damaged, 34 men dead, and many others injured. Although operated by the Navy, the *Liberty* was under operational control of the National Security Agency (NSA). The ship never received several urgent radio messages from Washington to leave the combat area.

### 5. USS *PUEBLO*

The U.S. Navy spy ship *Pueblo* (AGER 2) was boarded and captured by North Korean forces on January 23, 1968, some 12 miles off the coast of Wonsan. The *Pueblo* had been converted from an Army coastal cargo ship in 1966–1967 specifically for the collection of Electronic Intelligence (ELINT). There were 83 men aboard the ship at the time of her capture, including two civilian oceanographers. One sailor, who was wounded by North Korean gunfire, died while in captivity; the other 82 were held prisoner in North Korea for 11 months, finally being released after the U.S. Government apologized and admitted that the ship was in North Korean waters. Although operated by the Navy, the *Pueblo* was under operational control of the NSA.

## 6. EC-121 WARNING STAR

The largest loss of life in the shootdown of a spyplane occurred on April 15, 1969, when North Korean MiG fighters
shot down a U.S. Navy EC-121M Warning Star aircraft on an
ELINT mission over international waters off the coast of North
Korea. All 31 crewmen in the aircraft were killed. The EC-121
was a military version of the four-engine Super Constellation
transport aircraft.

## 7. RADAR OCEAN RECONNAISSANCE SATELLITES

The Soviet Radar Ocean Reconnaissance Satellite (RORSAT)
was the first satellite system orbited for ocean surveillance to
detect warships on the high seas. The Soviet Union began
tests of the system in 1967 and the first operational RORSATs
went into orbit in 1974. Two types of satellites were used in
tandem: Electronic Intelligence (ELINT) satellites that were
"passive" and sought to "lock on" to electronic signals ema-
nating from ships, especially radar transmissions; the 18,400-
pound ELINT satellites became operational about 1970. Pairs
of ELINT satellites were coordinated with a single RORSAT,
guiding the latter to a suspected target ship. The 10,000-pound
RORSAT could then use active radar to precisely locate and
target Western warships. Later RORSAT satellites could send
targeting data directly to missile-armed aircraft, surface ships,
and submarines as well as to ground stations. The large power
requirements for the RORSAT's radar were provided by a small
nuclear reactor that was fueled by some 110 pounds of en-
riched uranium ($U_{235}$) to produce up to ten kilowatts of power
for some 90 to 120 days in space.

## 8. THE EP-X SPYPLANE

The most famous—or infamous—spyplane in history was
the Lockheed U-2, flown by the U.S. Central Intelligence
Agency and the U.S. Air Force. In 1973–1974, the U.S. Navy

modified two U-2R aircraft to the U-2/EP-X configuration for evaluation for a possible ocean surveillance role. The designation indicated Electronic Patrol-eXperimental. During the evaluation the planes were fitted with a modified forward-looking radar for detecting surface ships and periscopes or snorkels of submerged submarines, and an infrared detection capability. The U-2/EP-X was to link its radar to surface ships under a program known as Outlaw Hawk. Other sensors, including satellite and land-based, were to be linked to a command center ashore and, subsequently, fitted in the carrier *Kitty Hawk* (CVA 63). During the Outlaw Hawk exercise involving the *Kitty Hawk*, the carrier steamed from San Diego to Pearl Harbor, with the U-2s flying from California. The U-2/EP-X concept died because of high costs and the promised effectiveness of satellites for ocean surveillance. Lockheed, ever hopeful of an enlarged U-2 program, also proposed its 315B design, a two-seat U-2 variant that would carry Condor anti-ship missiles under its wings. Another "payload" envisioned for U-2s in this period was a pair of unmanned or drone aircraft that would be released to serve as decoys for missiles fired against the U-2. No U-2 variant entered naval service, although CIA aircraft did operate them from aircraft carriers.

### 9. USS *HALIBUT*

The U.S. nuclear-propelled submarine *Halibut* (SSGN 587) was built to launch the Regulus land-attack cruise missile. After the shift to ballistic missiles as the U.S. sea-based deterrent force, the *Halibut*, originally completed in 1960, was reconfigured for special missions—the clandestine location and recovery of underwater objects. The *Halibut* and later special mission submarines gained public notoriety when it was revealed that they were employed to "tap" into Soviet seafloor communications cables. (Those clandestine operations were revealed to the Soviets in January 1980 by Ronald Pelton, a former employee of the National Security Agency.) Also, the *Halibut* was employed to tow a seafloor camera system that located the remains of a Soviet *Golf II*-class ballistic missile submarine that sank in the North Pacific in 1968, and was partially salvaged by a CIA operation employing the heavy lift ship *Glomar Explorer*.

## 10. "WHISKEY ON THE ROCKS"

During the Cold War, navies of the Western Alliance (NATO) and the Soviet Union employed submarines to spy out secrets. One of the most notable events of these operations occurred on October 27, 1981, when a Soviet diesel-electric submarine of the *Whiskey* class ran aground at Torumskär, near the Karlskrona naval base in southern Sweden. The submarine remained "high and dry" for several days until pulled into deep water by Swedish naval craft. While the Soviets prevented Swedish officials from inspecting the submarine's torpedoes, external radiation monitoring confirmed that the craft carried nuclear-armed torpedoes. A crew of 56 manned the submarine.

# Hybrids and Hermaphrodites

The development of new technologies—especially the large steel ships, aircraft, submarines, and big guns—led many designers and tactical planners to envision ways of combining those weapons. Long before the helicopter developed and small flight decks became a common warship feature, battleships and cruisers were envisioned with large flight decks, and submarines with aircraft and battleship guns.

## 1. THE LARGE LIGHT CRUISER *FURIOUS*

British First Sea Lord Adm. Jackie Fisher craved speed. The battle cruiser, a ship as big or bigger than a battleship, armed with battleship guns but lightly armored to save weight for more machinery to produce higher speeds, was his idea. Another plan he came up with was an invasion of Germany from the Baltic Sea. To do this he needed ships with big guns but shallow draft. The "large light cruisers" *Glorious* and *Courageous* were one result—large ships, each with two 15-inch twin gun turrets. Even larger was the *Furious*, which was to become the world's only ship armed with an 18-inch gun. She was to have carried two big guns, but during her construction Fisher left office and it was decided to fit the new ship with a flying off deck forward for aircraft. The *Furious* was completed in 1918 with the enormous 18-inch gun mounted aft in a single turret aft and the "flying-off deck" forward. She was the first aviation "hermaphrodite." (The *Furious* was later converted to a full-deck carrier, as were the *Courageous* and *Glorious*.)

## 2. THE CRUISER-AIRCRAFT CARRIER *VINDICTIVE*

The *Vindictive* started life as a light cruiser, laid down in 1916. But excitement over the conversion of the *Furious* led to a similar conversion of the smaller ship, which was completed in 1918. Fitted with flying-off decks fore and aft but retaining her cruiser superstructure and funnels amidships, she missed World War I but took part in several Baltic operations against the Bolsheviks after the war. After a year's service she was laid up and eventually converted into a training cruiser, losing her flying decks but becoming the first Royal Navy ship fitted with an aircraft-launching catapult.

## 3. BRITISH *M*-CLASS SUBMARINE MONITORS

Early British submarine designers gained a reputation for trying unique technologies, and the *M*-class submarines of World War I were no exception. Faced with torpedo ranges of barely over half a mile, planners thought the answer to longer range might be a battleship gun, which would provide devastating power at ranges of several miles. Three large submarines named *M1*, *M2*, and *M3* were built late in World War I, each carrying a single 12-inch gun—by far the largest gun ever fitted to a submarine. The subs were intended to bombard targets along the European coastline controlled by the Germans. The *M1* actually fired a few rounds in combat. The gun was fired near the surface, with several feet of the barrel and a periscope the only parts of the submarine protruding above the water. The submarine had to surface to reload. Somewhat surprisingly, the ungainly looking submarines had ill-fated careers. The *M1* was sunk in collision in 1925; the others lost their big guns with the *M2* being modified to carry a floatplane, and sank accidentally; the *M3* was turned into a minelayer and was scrapped before too long.

## 4. THE CRUISER-SEAPLANE CARRIER-MINELAYER *GOTLAND*

The small but efficient Swedish Navy always looked to combine multiple capabilities in its warships, and in the late 1920s a unique ship was conceived that could act as a cruiser, seaplane carrier and minelayer. The 5,500-ton *Gotland* that was completed in late 1934 looked like a cruiser forward, with a 6-inch twin gun turret and two additional 6-inch guns in casemates, with another twin 6-inch turret amidships. From amidships aft she was a seaplane carrier. A 65½-foot compressed air catapult was fitted with six floatplanes being carried (she could accommodate more planes, but they weren't available). After alighting on the water near the ship, a large crane would hoist the planes back aboard. And, she could carry a large number of mines. The *Gotland* garnered a good bit of international admiration, but didn't keep her aircraft long, and in 1944 she emerged from a refit with her catapult and aircraft gone, replaced by anti-aircraft guns. She was converted to a training cruiser in the mid-1950s and scrapped in 1963.

## 5. BATTLESHIP "X"

The idea of building a combination battleship-carrier or large cruiser-carrier was popular during the 1920s and 1930s in the United States and Europe, and when the Soviet Union approached the American design firm of Gibbs and Cox about designing a state-of-the-art battleship, naval architect William Francis Gibbs responded with one of the most intriguing capital ship designs ever proposed. Gibbs proposed an enormous, 74,000-ton behemoth, over 1,000 feet long, carrying four triple turrets with a dozen 16-inch guns. The superstructure and funnel were offset to starboard to allow a hangar and flight deck fitted amidships, capable of accommodating 36 wheeled aircraft and four seaplanes. When the project became public in 1938 it was designated "Ship X," and some observers wanted the U.S. Navy to build similar ships. But the State Department declared the size of the ship illegally outstripped the London Naval Treaty that was then in force (the Soviets were not party to the treaty, but the United States was) and Gibbs proposed a somewhat smaller design for the United States. But for several reasons—including the Soviet invasion of Poland in 1939—the ships were never built for either navy.

### 6. MERCHANT AIRCRAFT CARRIERS

As the Battle of the Atlantic wore on in the early 1940s, it became evident that the U.S. and British Navies required more aircraft carriers for convoy escort. U.S. shipyards were turned to producing large numbers of escort or "jeep" carrier aircraft carriers and the British came up with another wartime expediency: installing flight decks on top of working merchant ships. The merchant ship hull retained its cargo capacity while the aviation portion of the ships could operate three or four Swordfish submarine-hunting biplanes. The first ship converted was the *Empire MacAlpine*, a grain carrier. A flight deck and a one-airplane hangar were installed while the ship was still under construction, and she went to sea in April 1943 carrying four Swordfish. Tankers also were converted, although with no room for even a tiny hangar they could carry only three or four aircraft. Manning was a mixed effort as well: the civilian merchant crews ran the ship, Royal Navy sailors maintained and flew the aircraft, and soldiers operated the ships' few defensive weapons. The MACs were reasonably successful, and after the war the survivors were reconverted to standard merchant configuration.

## 7. JAPANESE ARMY "COMBO-SHIPS"

It's a transport! A landing ship! An aircraft carrier! The Japanese Army converted three merchant ships during World War II that were able to fly off aircraft and carry troops and landing craft. The *Akitsu Maru*, *Nigitsu Maru*, and *Kumano Maru* weren't meant to be operational aircraft carriers, but instead were to fly off their aircraft to land ashore. The ships retained something of their cargo-liner appearance with a flight deck extending over about four-fifths of their length. The aft area was left open for a hatch and handling boom. The first two ships were sunk by U.S. submarines shortly after completion in 1944, while the *Kumano Maru*, completed only a few months before the war ended, survived to be scrapped in 1951. The Japanese Army also flew autogiros from some of these ships to search for enemy submarines.

## 8. HERMAPHRODITE BATTLESHIPS AND CRUISERS

The Japanese aircraft carrier force suffered a major blow early in June 1942 when four of its six large carriers were sunk at the Battle of Midway. Having relied so much on carrier aviation during the first six months of World War II, the Imperial Navy was desperate to restore at least some of the lost flying capacity, and conversion plans were drawn up for all ten of the fleet's older battleships. After much discussion, two older six-turret battleships, the *Ise* and *Hyuga*, were taken in hand for conversion. The aftermost pair of 14-inch gun turrets were removed and replaced with a hangar topped by a flight deck. The original intention was for the ships to carry conventional D4Y Judy dive bombers, launched by two catapults and intended to land either on other aircraft carriers or ashore. In service, though, only about 11 float planes were carried by each ship. Another victim of American dive bombers at Midway was the heavily damaged cruiser *Mogami*, and she too was converted, with a long flying deck, but no hangar, re-placing her two after 8-inch gun turrets. None of the conver-sions were effective in the carrier role. The *Mogami* was sunk in October 1944 at the Battle of Leyte Gulf, while both hy-brid battleships were sunk in harbor in Japan by U.S. aircraft in 1945.

### 9. SOVIET InnOVATIOnS

The advent of short takeoff/vertical landing (STOVL) aircraft in the 1960s caused some warship designers to envision air-craft-carrying ships that would retain missile cruiser features. The resulting concept, dubbed a "through-deck cruiser," was subsequently developed by Britain and the Soviet Union. The British version evolved into the *Invincible* class of three ships completed in the 1980s, but the ships were small aircraft car-riers and lacked cruiser capabilities. Not so for the Soviets, who first went to sea in the 1960s with the small, 15,500-ton *Moskva* and *Leningrad,* which were cruisers forward and helicopter carriers aft. The four much larger *Kiev*-class ships, 36,000 tons standard, completed in the 1970s and 1980s, were truly mixed-use ships. While an angled deck capable of handling helicopters and Yak-38 Forger VSTOL jets extended for about two-thirds of the ship's length, the ships carried an impressive missile battery forward, with long-range anti-ship and anti-aircraft missiles forward as well as anti-submarine weapons and a massive array of electronic systems. Four of the *Kiev*s were built—each with significant improvements over her predecessor. They were among the first ships to be taken out of service after the fall of the Soviet Union in December 1991. One ended up as an "amusement park" in China, an-other, not serviceable, sits in a Chinese port, and one is being converted for service in the Indian Navy.

## 10. THE DESTROYER-AIRCRAFT CARRIER

The Japanese constitution of post-World War II renounced forever the idea of war on other nations—the primary reason the country's military forces are called self-defense forces rather than the navy, army or air force. Countries that suffered at the hands of the Japanese remain wary of signs of military resurgence, and an aircraft carrier might be considered one of those signs. In 2008 the Japanese Navy commissioned the *Hyuga*, an 18,000-ton destroyer that looks like a small aircraft carrier. The Japanese claim that the ship is a destroyer, fitted with a full flight deck and hangar (with two elevators) to operate only helicopters. But the ship is larger than the small aircraft carriers operated by Italy, Spain, and Thailand. Japanese defense analysts admit the ship will be able to operate AV-8 Harrier jump-jets as well as the F-35B STOVL version of the new U.S. Joint Strike Fighter. And, the ship is armed with the Aegis air defense system. The Japanese plan to build four of the ships. At the *Hyuga*'s launching in August 2007 sensitivities were evidenced by the Japanese government's refusal to allow video or images of the new ship to circulate. Nevertheless, critics in several Asian countries have criticized the Japanese for building such a provocative warship. It might be coincidence that the ship's name harks back to one of the World War II hybrid battleships.

# Amphibious Ships

## 1. **THE BLOODY** *RIVER CLYDE*

The Romans had used small, specialized ships to carry their legions and horses for invasions, including their landings in England in 55 BC. In the early 1700s, the Russians under Peter the Great carried out numerous landings with specialized craft in their campaigns against the Swedes in the Gulf of Finland. The first "modern" amphibious ship was the British *River Clyde*, a steel-hull collier modified for use in the landings at Cape Helles beach in the Dardanelles campaign of 1915. Gangways were fitted to the ship's sides and "sally ports" were cut into her sides, and sandbags were mounted to protect her superstructure from Turkish gunfire. Some 2,000 British troops were embarked in the ship. On the morning of April 25, the *River Clyde* was grounded at Cape Helles. Instantly the Turks opened fire from the heights with rifles and machine guns. Although she was grounded, the water was too deep for the *River Clyde*'s troops to wade ashore. A barge was brought alongside to bridge the gap to the beach. Still, some 700 troops in the landing ship were killed or wounded. Most of the survivors got ashore safely that night.

## 2. THE FIRST LARGE LANDING SHIP

The U.S. Navy is best known for developing and building the world's largest modern fleet of amphibious ships, but it was the Imperial Japanese Army that first thought up the idea of the landing ship transport. In the early 1930s the Japanese Navy was asked to build the ship, named the *Shinshu Maru*, and she was no half-hearted design. Built in 1933, she was big–12,000 tons, nearly 500 feet long—and relatively fast at 19 knots. The ship was designed to carry 20 small but fully loaded, 46-foot Daihatsu landing craft, and the Army even planned to install catapults to launch small floatplanes. While still under construction, the Navy took over the project and completed the ship without the catapults. After 1941 the Japanese converted two similar ships from merchant hulls.

## 3. THE LANDING SHIP TANK

The iconic American LST was first conceived by the British, and an Englishman sketched out the first design on a table napkin. Having been thrown out of Europe by June 1940, the Brits were looking forward to the day they that would return and realized they needed a ship capable of landing a tank directly on a beach. The earliest LSTs were converted oil tankers, but Britain lacked the industrial capacity to build enough ships and the Americans soon asked to help. Realizing a good thing, the U.S. shipyards eventually built 1,052 LSTs, the first completed in December 1942. Dubbed "Large Slow Targets"—because of their top speed of 11 knots—they nevertheless displayed remarkable survivability when damaged. Only 26 were lost in combat, although landing beaches were very dangerous areas with another 13 the victims of heavy weather. LSTs soon became one of the most useful ships developed during World War II. They appeared in every theater of war and dozens were converted to other uses such as tenders and repair ships, and casualty evacuation transports. Hundreds were sold off after 1945 for military and commercial use. Cheaply built and intended to last only for the duration of the war, a great many remained active for decades. In the Korean and Vietnam Wars they even served as helicopter ships. Several are still in service today.

## 4. SIZE ISN'T EVERYTHING

Although it took great fleets to carry out the Allied amphibious assaults that began in the second half of 1942, most troops hit the beach in a small craft just short of 36 feet in length. It was derived from an earlier landing craft designed by the indomitable Andrew Higgins, a New Orleans boatbuilder. The landing craft, vehicle personnel or LCVP carried about 36 troops or four tons of cargo, including a jeep; it could slide up a sloping beach, drop its bow ramp and get everyone out in less than 20 seconds—key factors when hitting the beach in the face of determined enemy fire. Thousands of LCVPs were built during the war. Similar in concept to the Japanese 46-foot Diahatsu, in various forms the LCVP remains in use today in several navies.

## 5. AMPHIBIOUS FORCE FLAGSHIPS

The ever-expanding Allied assaults of World War II showed that putting an army or force of marines ashore directly into combat was an incredibly complex affair. Command and control became a very serious issue, with dozens of land, sea and air commanders needing to communicate with and direct their forces at the same time. A general bringing his staff aboard a cruiser or battleship could not find space to work his maps, plots, and communications, and the ship might be needed elsewhere in her warship role. It was soon realized

A Pacific island hosts four landing craft tanks (LCT), a landing ship medium (LSM), and a landing ship tank (LST). Scores of additional "amphibs" are offshore. *U.S. Navy*

that a specialized ship was needed. Enter the *Bulolo*, a British "headquarters ship" converted early in 1942, soon joined by a series of American amphibious flagships. As the need continued to grow, more ships were converted, including six large U.S. Coast Guard cutters, and the concept migrated to smaller ships on lower tactical levels. Fifteen large, 12,800-ton merchant hull-amphibious force flagship (AGC) conversions had staff accommodations for some 55 officers and 580 enlisted men in addition to their crews. After World War II the idea matured into the modern command ship, and in the late 1960s the U.S. Navy constructed two built-for-the-purpose amphibious force flagships, the *Blue Ridge* (AGC, later LCC 19) and *Mount Whitney* (AGC/LCC 20). Both ships remain in service as fleet flagships as this book went to press.

### 6. MOST BANG FOR THE BUCK: THE LCS(L)(3)

The diminutive landing craft support (narge) Mark 3 of World War II lacked a sexy name (and, like most landing ships they were given only numbers, not names), but perhaps packed more punch per pound into 387 tons than any other ship type. Born of a need to get more powerful firepower right up close on the beach during an amphibious assault, the design of the LCS(L)(3) was modified from an existing landing ship. With a draft of less than five feet forward and less than seven feet aft, the 158-foot-long ships—dubbed "Mighty Midgets"— carried a twin 40-mm Bofors gun mount forward along with a single 40-mm or 3-inch gun, several 20-mm Oerlikon guns, .50-caliber machine guns, and ten rocket launchers. The LCS(L)(3) was meant to accompany troops in the first wave of an assault and 130 were built in 1944–1945. Many were transferred after the war to France, where they were used in Indochina and many eventually were acquired by the Republic of Vietnam (South Vietnam). A number also were transferred after the war, ironically, to Japan.

The larger "cousin" to the LCS(L)(3) was the landing ship, medium (rocket) or LSM(R), which carried a 5-inch gun and a heavier rocket battery. These ships stood farther offshore as they blasted away at Japanese-held islands with 5-inch-diameter rockets.

### 7. THE ODD DUCK

When in late 1941 the American Car Corporation of Buffalo, New York, first offered its "swimming truck" to the U.S. Army, few officers realized the odd little craft would still be a familiar American tourist vehicle in the early 21st Century. The Army considered the new vehicle the amphibious equivalent of its standard 2½-ton truck, and soon DUKWs were a familiar sight in most Allied landing fleets. The designation came from Army designation practice, where D indicated 1942, U stood for amphibious, K meant front-wheel drive, and W rear-wheel drive. The letters rapidly turned simply into "duck"—which happily also rhymed with truck. Hundreds were sold post-war, and many were converted into tourist vehicles in cities on harbors or rivers.

The U.S. Marines, faced with more treacherous coral islands to assault in the Pacific, used tracked amphibious vehicles designated LVT, and LVTA if they mounted a major gun. These vehicles could carry a squad, unloaded through a rear ramp, and could move up onto the land to serve as lightly armored troop transport and cargo vehicles.

## 8. ATTACK TRANSPORTS AND CARGO SHIPS

Specialized transports and cargo ships to unload combat troops for an amphibious assault were a distinctly World War II innovation, and the U.S. Navy put a great deal of effort into combining military and cargo requirements into a single hull with a couple hundred of these ships being built. Attack cargo ships (AKA) and attack transports (APA) differed from standard ships of their type by being modified to carry cargo in the order to be unloaded, not the most efficient stowage procedure, and to rapidly unload cargo and troops into landing craft (many of which were stowed on their decks). Large cranes made them independent of shore facilities to unload cargo and vehicles. These unsung warriors were invaluable for the numerous Allied assaults of World War II and in the Korean War.

## 9. THE FIRST AIR-CUSHION LANDING CRAFT

Although the concept of a craft riding on a cushion of air dated at least from the 19th Century, air-cushioned craft gained practicality during the 1960s, when such vehicles were envisioned as replacements for conventional civilian ferries and for small combat craft (three prototypes were used by U.S.

forces in the Vietnam War). Military planners also liked the ability to ride right up over the beach and discharge cargo onto dry land, and the British, Soviets and Americans rushed to develop an operational craft. Britain's Saunders-Roe company produced the first practical hovercraft, the *SR.N1*, which crossed the English Channel in 1959. Widely known as "hovercraft," the concept traded carrying capacity for speed and agility. They also are extremely noisy but can rapidly deliver cargo, tanks, and trucks from ships to the beach. The U.S. Navy's landing craft air-cushion (LCAC) can carry more than 60 tons at a speed of 50 knots when "on the cushion." The Russian Navy has built even larger air-cushion landing craft, some being able to carry more than 300 troops or three main battle tanks or ten armored personnel carriers; their top speed is over 60 knots.

## 10. THE LARGEST AMPHIBIOUS SHIPS

The U.S. Navy's amphibious assault ships of the *Tarawa* (LHA 1), *Wasp* (LHD 1), and *Makin Island* (LHD 8) classes are among the largest warships ever built, being outpaced only by the largest aircraft carriers and battleships. All displace about 30,000 tons standard, making them larger than World War II carriers of the *Essex* (CV 9) class. These amphibious ships, more than 800 feet long, can operate about 30 large helicopters and VSTOL aircraft, can embark more than 1,500 troops, and most have a floodable docking well that can accommodate landing craft or amphibious vehicles. Several other navies have recently constructed similar ships, although not as large as the U.S. giants.

# Weird Ships

## 1. TURTLE SHIPS

The world's first armored ships were not the Union *Monitor* and Confederate *Virginia* (neé *Merrimack*) of the American Civil War, but the Korean "turtle ships." These strange-looking craft—known as Geobukseon or Kobukson in Korean—were large warships built during the Joseon Dynasty from the early 15th Century up until the 19th Century. The Korean Adm. Yi Sun-sin is credited with designing and building the craft, which had wooden hulls and a covered upper deck, which in turn was sheathed with iron plates and spikes, the latter to deter boarders. Yi had three to five turtle ships built, with the first being launched on March 27, 1592. This type of warship continued in Korean service over the years, and by 1782 there were at least 40 of them in Korean service. Their armament consisted of several cannons. Rowers propelled the turtle ships although a single mast and square sail were provided, which could be raised and furled from within the ship (i.e., no need to send men on deck). Another unusual feature of some turtle ships was a dragon head mounted on the bow that emitted sulfur gas to hide the craft's movement from the enemy in short-range fighting. The dragon heads were large enough for a cannon to fit inside. It was also a form of psychological warfare, the dragon symbol intended to strike fear into the hearts of Japanese sailors. The turtle ships were about 100 to 120 feet long. Yi employed them during his several victories over Japanese invasions of Korea (1592–1598), in which they inflicted major damage against Japanese warships.

## 2. POPOVKAS

The most unusual big-gun ships ever built were probably the Russian "circular ironclads," popularly known as "Popovkas" after their designer, Rear Adm. A.A. Popov. His goal was to develop a coastal warship of small dimensions that could carry a heavy gun battery and be a very stable gun platform. Often described as the "ugliest warships ever built," the hulls of the *Novgorod* and the larger *Vice Admiral Popov* were circular when viewed from overhead. They were almost unmaneuverable, slow (seven knots), and were vulnerable to plunging gunfire. Even in moderate seas they pitched and rolled excessively. And, the off-axis recoil of their main guns imparted a centrifugal rotation to the ship. The ships were driven by six steam reciprocating engines, each with its own propeller shaft. Their main battery consisted of two 11-inch guns. Completed in the 1870s, both ships served in the Danube Flotilla during the Russo-Turkish War of 1877–1878. They were redesignated as "coastal defense armor-clad ships" in 1892, and were used as storeships from 1903 until they were broken up for scrap in 1912.

## 3. MONITORS

The name monitor—for a warship with a few large guns, usually intended for coastal operations—is derived from the USS *Monitor* of Civil War fame. Called the "cheese box on a raft," the *Monitor* was built in record time by engineer John Ericsson for the Union Navy in response to rumors that the Confederate States had an ironclad warship that could defeat all wooden

Union warships. The low-lying *Monitor* had a round, rotating turret with two 11-inch Dahlgren smoothbore guns. She was completed on February 25, 1862, and fought the *Virginia* (ex-*Merrimack*) to a standstill at Hampton Roads, Virginia, on March 8. The *Virginia* withdrew and the Confederates later scuttled the ironclad. It was history's first engagement of armored warships.

## 4. FLOATING DRY DOCKS

As the U.S. fleet began operating in the Philippines after the defeat of the Spanish in 1898, there was the need for a large dry dock to service U.S. ships. The so-called *Dewey* dry dock was built in 1905 near Baltimore, Maryland, and towed to Manila Bay in 1906. Subsequently, in World War II the U.S. Navy built scores of floating dry docks, some—the Navy's multi-section advanced base sectional docks (ASBD)—could lift a battleship or aircraft carrier. These docks, the ABSDs in sections, could be towed to advance bases, alleviating the need for damaged ships to return to American bases for repairs. Floating dry docks are still in use in several navies.

## 5. THE CATAPULT SHIP

Beginning in the 1930s the U.S. Navy made wide use of flying boat patrol aircraft to support the fleet, primarily by scouting for the enemy with the PBY Catalina and PBM Mariners. To launch the heavy flying boats in rough water conditions, in 1940–1941 the Navy built a "catapult lighter" (designated AVC 1). The ship displaced 5,860 tons and was $423^5/_6$ feet long—larger than a destroyer. The AVC 1 was to be towed into forward harbors where, when needed, she could "fire off" large seaplanes. The development of rocket canisters to help aircraft takeoff—called JATO units—alleviated the need for the ship and she was discarded without having been used operationally.

## 6. ICEBERG AIRCRAFT CARRIERS

A British development, the concept of an "iceberg" aircraft carrier was intended to help compensate for the shortage of aircraft carriers in 1942. Scientist Geoffrey Pyke proposed that floating platforms be constructed from a mixture of sea water and sawdust, frozen together to make a material he called "Pykrete." Experiments demonstrated that as Pykrete melted, the fibrous content quickly formed a furry outer surface that acted as an insulator and greatly retarded the melting process. It was considerably stronger than normal ice. Experiments showed that bomb and torpedo damage to such a craft would be minor and, if above water, could be easily repaired. A scale model of an "iceberg carrier" was built in Canada. Given the code name Habbakuk—recalling a minor Hebrew prophet of the Bible—the proposed Pykrete carrier would be the largest floating structure ever attempted, displacing more than two million tons with a length of some 2,000 feet. A power plant of only 20,000 shaft horsepower was expected to propel the "craft" up to 6.5 knots when Habbakuk had a clean hull. But the high cost of such a venture, the need for special construction facilities, and the availability of more aircraft carriers put an end to a most unusual proposal.

## 7. RADAR PICKET SUBMARINES

Radar does not function underwater. Still, radar picket submarines were important undersea craft in the years immediately after World War II. During the invasion of Okinawa in April 1945 the Japanese used kamikaze (suicide) attacks to strike U.S. ships. Radar-equipped destroyers were placed to give early warning of the attacking planes and they too became victims of the savage air attacks. The U.S. Navy conceived the concept of radar picket submarines (SSR), which could stand out from the invasion ships to give early warning of air attacks. They would then submerge to escape the approaching aircraft. After the war the U.S. Navy converted several diesel-electric submarines to the SSR role, and built three new radar submarines—two diesel-electric and the USS *Triton* (SSRN 586), a nuclear-propelled submarine 447½ feet long, at the time the world's largest undersea craft.

## 8. PRESIDENTIAL COMMAND SHIPS

Throughout history, admirals commanding squadrons and fleets have used available warships for their flagships. In the sailing era their staffs were small and communication was mainly by signal flags ruin up ships' masts. But by World War II the admirals had scores of staff personnel—intelligence officers, communications specialists, cryptologists, and others. And, the communications equipment required more space and antennas. Accordingly, after World War II the U.S. Navy began converting cruisers to fleet flagships. The most impressive was the heavy cruiser *Northampton* (CA 125), a 13,000-ton warship left unfinished at the end of the war. She was rebuilt and completed as a fleet command ship (CLC 1) in 1953. Later she was reconfigured as an emergency command ship for the president in the event of a nuclear attack (changed to CC 1). A small aircraft carrier was also converted to that role and a third ship was planned. Plans called for the president and senior civil and military officials to be flown out to the ships by helicopter in the event of a nuclear attack.

## 9. SUBMARINE LSTS

Beginning in World War II the Soviet Navy sponsored the design of large underwater cargo ships and transports, initially to get reinforcements into coastal cities besieged by the Germans. Interest continued after the war and, eventually, nuclear-propelled transport submarines were designed. The ultimate design developed for the Soviet Navy was Project

717, a giant transport submarine with nuclear propulsion that could carry 800 marines and 20 amphibious tanks and armored personnel carriers. They would be unloaded in shallow water over twin ramps that extended from the submarine. The underwater giant was to displace 18,300 tons on the surface with a length of 623½ feet. The design for Project 717 was completed in October 1971 and preparations were made at the Severodvinsk shipyard in the Arctic to begin construction of several submarines of this type. But the project was stillborn, as the massive building halls at the Severodvinsk shipyard were needed for construction of the large Typhoon ballistic missile submarines.

### 10. THE *GLOMAR EXPLORER*

The Soviet diesel-electric, missile-armed submarine *K-129* sank suddenly in the mid-Pacific with all of her crew of 98 men being lost. The U.S. Navy's sound surveillance system (SOSUS) detected the submarine's breaking up sounds. A seemingly fantastic effort was undertaken to locate the exact position of the sunken sub and to lift her from a depth of three miles, many times deeper than any craft of that size had been salvaged. With the cooperation of aviation industrialist, film producer, and eccentric millionaire Howard Hughes—who was used as the cover story for the project—the Central Intelligence Agency built the salvage ship *Glomar Explorer* to lift the submarine into a hidden "hangar" within the ship. After the U.S. submarine *Halibut* (SSN 587) clandestinely located the *K-129*, the salvage ship—under the cover story of searching for manganese nodules—was able to lift a portion of the stricken submarine in 1974. The *Glomar Explorer* was then laid up in reserve—possibly awaiting another unusual assignment.

# Aircraft

### 1. FASTEST JET-PROPELLED AIRCRAFT

The fastest jet-propelled aircraft in naval service was the McDonnell F4H Phantom (first flight 1958), a multi-mission fighter designed for carrier operations. The Phantom's speed was in excess of Mach 2—more than twice the speed of sound. The only other Mach 2 carrier-based aircraft was the North American A3J Vigilante, a nuclear strike aircraft, subsequently used in the reconnaissance role. The Phantom set several speed and climb-to-altitude records. (These aircraft were re-designated in 1962 the F-4 and A-5, respectively.)

### 2. FASTEST PISTON-ENGINE AIRCRAFT

The Grumman F8F Bearcat (first flight 1944) was the fastest U.S. Navy piston-engine aircraft. Developed as a low-weight fighter, it did not see combat in World War II, but was used by the French in Indochina. The F8F-1 was rated at 421 m.p.h. Several privately owned Bearcats set speed records; the *Rare Bear*, with an uprated engine, set a three-kilometer speed record of 528.33 m.p.h. in 1990.

### 3. FASTEST SEAPLANES

The world's fastest seaplane was the Martin P6M SeaMaster flying boat (first flight 1955). It was intended for nuclear strike, aerial minelaying, and photo reconnaissance. Powered by four turbojet engines, the P6M exceeded 600 m.p.h. on test flights. Twelve of the flying boat bombers were completed; however, the P6M program was cancelled in 1959 to help fund the Polaris missile program.

The fastest jet-propelled seaplane to enter service is the Beriev A-40 Mermaid, a twin turbofan-powered flying boat that has had limited Russian service, primarily for the search and rescue role. The plane's cruise speed is 435 m.p.h. (The aircraft also has the designation Be-42.)

### 4. LARGEST LAND AIRCRAFT

The largest land-based aircraft to be built specifically for naval service was the Lockheed R6O-1 Constitution (first flight 1946). With a gross weight of almost 190,000 pounds, powered by four-piston engines, the Constitution could carry 40 tons of cargo or 170 passengers or 200 troops in addition to a 12-man crew. Although only two prototypes were built, they did enter operational service; both were retired in 1953. (Their designation was changed from R6O to R6V in 1950.)

### 5. LARGEST SEAPLANES

Unquestionably, the largest government-sponsored seaplane ever built was the so-called "Spruce Goose"—the largest aircraft built in World War II, although it did not fly until two years after the war and then for only *one minute* on November 2, 1947. Despite its popular name, it was not made of spruce. The giant aircraft was developed by Howard Hughes (of *Glomar Explorer* fame, above), and was the product of a brief collaboration of Hughes and shipbuilder Henry J. Kaiser that sought to produce a "flying cargo ship" that could move troops and weapons overseas without the risk of losses to enemy submarines. With an estimated gross weight of 300,000 pounds, it was to carry 65 tons of cargo or 750 troops or 350 litter patients.

The largest "military" seaplane was the Martin P6M SeaMaster (first flight 1955), which was expected to weigh up to 190,000 pounds fully loaded.

The world's largest operational seaplanes and the U.S. Navy's largest aircraft of the World War II era were the Martin-built Mars flying boats. The four-engine prototype XPB2M-1 (first flight 1942) was reconfigured as a cargo aircraft and became the model for five large JRM flying boats. They could carry 132 troops, or 84 litters plus 10 medical attendants, or 11 tons of cargo; for short runs they could carry 300 passengers. The single JRM-2—slightly larger than her sister planes— had a gross takeoff weight of 165,000 pounds and could carry 16 tons of cargo.

## 6. FIRST SHIPBOARD LANDING

The first aircraft landing aboard a ship was made by civilian pilot Eugene Ely flying a Curtiss pusher biplane aboard the U.S. Navy armored cruiser *Pennsylvania* (CA 4) in San Francisco Bay on January 18, 1911. After lunch, Ely took off and flew back to shore. Capt. Charles F. Pond, commanding officer of the *Pennsylvania*, declared, "This is the most important landing of a bird since the dove flew back to the Ark." Later he reported on the flight to the Navy Department: "I declare to place myself on record as positively assured of the importance of the aeroplane in future naval warfare, certainly for scouting purposes."

## 7. FIRST SHIPBOARD TAKEOFF

The first takeoff from a ship occurred on November 14, 1910, when Eugene Ely took off in a Curtiss pusher biplane from the U.S. Navy light cruiser *Birmingham* (CL 2) in Hampton Roads (Chesapeake Bay), Virginia.

## 8. LONGEST-RANGE AIRCRAFT

A Lockheed XP2V-1 Neptune (first flight 1945) accomplished the longest non-refueled flight by a naval aircraft in September 1946. That twin piston-engine aircraft, the *Truculent Turtle*, was piloted by Comdr. Thomas D. Davies, when it flew 11,236 miles from Perth, Australia, to Columbus, Ohio, in 55 hours, 17 minutes. (The Neptune's distance record was broken by a U.S. Air Force B-52H Stratofortress that flew 12,532 miles in 1962–some 16 years later.)

## 9. LONGEST SERVING AIRCRAFT

The Lockheed P3V Orion (first flight 1961) has been in first-line service longer than any other specialized naval aircraft. The maritime patrol/anti-submarine aircraft, a four-turboprop aircraft derived from the commercial Lockheed Electra, entered U.S. Navy service with Patrol Squadrons 8 and 44 in August 1962, and continues in service with the U.S. Navy and several other air forces.

## 10. AIRCRAFT PRODUCED IN LARGEST NUMBERS

The U.S. Navy and Marine Corps as well as the Army Air Forces both flew the Consolidated B-24 Liberator—naval designation PB4Y-1. It was produced in larger numbers than any other U.S. combat aircraft with 18,190 built from 1939 to 1945, with 977 going directly to the U.S. Navy and Marine Corps. The Chance Vought F4U Corsair (first flight 1940) had the largest production run of a specialized naval aircraft: From 1940 to December 1952, the Chance Vought, Brewster, and Goodyear firms produced 15,056 aircraft, including 2,486 that went directly to other countries. Additional Corsairs went to other air forces after U.S. service. Corsairs were designated F4U and AU (Chance Vought), F3A (Brewster), and FG (Goodyear).

# Most Famous Aircraft

## 1. NC-4

The U.S. Navy's Curtiss-designed NC flying boat (first flight 1918) was developed for long-range anti-submarine operations against German U-boats. The NC-4 of this series was the first aircraft to fly across the Atlantic Ocean, albeit in stages. Completed too late for World War II, ten of the three-engine aircraft were produced by Curtiss and the Naval Aircraft Factory. Three of the aircraft attempted a trans-Atlantic flight in May 1919; only the NC-4 was successful. Commanded by Lt. Comdr. Albert C. Read, the aircraft flew from Newfoundland, to the Azores, to Lisbon, to Portsmouth, England.

## 2. SWORDFISH

The Fairey Swordfish (first flight 1934) was the principal British carrier-based bomber of early World War II and one of the most famous British warplanes of all time. The open-cockpit, biplane Swordfish was obsolete when the war began; it was far inferior in performance to the Japanese B5N1 torpedo bomber (Allied codename Kate) and the U.S. Navy's TBD Devastator torpedo plane. Still, flying from British carriers, Swordfish sank the Italian battle fleet at anchor at Taranto, stopped the German battleship *Bismarck*, and were responsible for sinking and damaging many other Axis ships and submarines. It was employed for scouting, anti-submarine warfare, and torpedo and dive-bombing attacks. The Swordfish was affectionately called the "Stringbag" after a wag, commenting on the variety of weapons the plane could carry, remarked, "No housewife on a shopping spree could cram a wider variety of articles into her stringbag."

### 3. A6M ZERO

The Mitsubishi A6M Zero (first flight 1939) was the outstanding Japanese fighter of the war. It demonstrated for the first time that a carrier-based aircraft (with folding wing sections) could have superiority over land-based contemporaries. Zero designer Jiro Horikoshi wrote that the Japanese Navy's requirements for the plane "seemed impossible to meet. If this

The Fairey Swordfish was one of the last two biplanes to operate from aircraft carriers—the other being the British Albacore torpedo plane. *Fleet Air Arm Museum*

airplane could be built, it certainly would be superior to the rest of the world's fighters." Horikoshi's design team met the requirements and for the first two years of the war in the Pacific the Zero was the best fighter in the theater. Not until the appearance of the U.S. Navy's F6F Hellcat in 1943 did the Allies have a fighter that could better the Zero under almost all combat conditions. The Zero was flown—as a fighter, dive bomber, and suicide aircraft—until the end of the war. The Allied codename for the Zero was "Zeke," but Zero was usually used (indicating the year of issue in the Japanese calendar, i.e., 2600.)

## 4. SBD DAUNTLESS

The Douglas SBD Dauntless scout-dive bomber (first flight XBT-1 1935) was probably the most effective dive bomber in naval history. U.S. Navy SBDs destroyed four Japanese aircraft carriers in a single day at the battle of Midway on June 4, 1942. Scores of other Japanese warships and merchant ships as well as a few submarines were sunk by SBDs. Although a carrier-based aircraft, the SBD's wings did not fold for carrier stowage. It was also flown by the Marine Corps and—with limited effectiveness—by the U.S. Army Air Forces as the A-24.

## 5. F4U CORSAIR

The Chance Vought F4U Corsair (first flight 1940) was in continuous production longer than any other World War II-era combat aircraft. The F4U Corsair was a large, powerful fighter. Flying from aircraft carriers and land bases, the F4U had a kill-to-loss ratio of 11:1 over Japanese aircraft with an estimated 1,400 enemy planes of all types destroyed by F4Us in the Pacific. It was a large, heavy aircraft compared to its Grumman-built counterparts. The aircraft was flown in large numbers by British and Commonwealth naval air arms as well as the French Navy; subsequently, several other air forces flew the Corsair. The plane was used aboard U.S. carriers in the Korean War and in the 1950s aboard French aircraft carriers during the Suez campaign.

### 6. F6F HELLCAT

The Grumman F6F Hellcat (first flight 1942) was the first U.S. fighter that could defeat the Japanese A6M Zero fighter under virtually all conditions. According to aviation historian William Green, "the appearance of the Hellcat in the late summer of 1943 changed the [combat] situation virtually overnight." The F6F was credited with 4,947 of the 6,477 enemy aircraft destroyed in the air by U.S. Navy carrier pilots. The principal fighter on the larger U.S. aircraft carriers from 1943 to 1945, the F6F was predominant in the carrier battles of the Marianas and Leyte Gulf. The aircraft was also flown in large numbers from British carriers.

### 7. AD SKYRAIDER

The Douglas AD Skyraider (first flight 1945) represented the ultimate in piston-engine attack aircraft and was probably the most versatile American-built aircraft in history. It saw extensive service with the U.S. Air Force, Navy, and Marine Corps as well as Britain, France, Cambodia, and South Vietnam. It was flown by U.S. forces in the Korean and Vietnam Wars. The Skyraider was also the world's first single-engine aircraft to carry a nuclear weapon. There were 28 possible configurations of the Skyraider, including attack, night/all-weather attack, airborne early warning (AEW), electronic countermeasures (ECM), transport, medical evacuation, tanker, photographic, anti-submarine, target-tug, drone control, and nuclear strike. Skyraider pilot and author Rosario ("Zip") Rausa wrote that the aircraft's "most distinctive characteristic . . . was its straightforward, uncomplicated design. Its unadorned style gave it an aura of simplicity and strength." (In 1962 the aircraft was redesignated A-1.)

## 8. A4D SKYHAWK

The Douglas A4D Skyhawk (first flight 1954) was in many respects the most remarkable nuclear strike aircraft produced by any nation. Entering service in 1955 as a U.S. carrier-based attack aircraft, the Skyhawk also served as a conventional strike, interdiction, and close air support aircraft in several air forces. And, U.S. and Israeli Skyhawk pilots were able to down MiG fighters. The Skyhawk was flown by the U.S. Navy and Marine Corps in the Vietnam War from both land bases and aircraft carriers, with 30 squadrons operating the aircraft in 1968. It was also employed by the Argentine Air Force against British forces in the 1982 Falklands conflict, by the Israel Air Force in several Middle East conflicts, and a few were flown by the Kuwaiti Air Force in the 1991 Gulf War. It served in the U.S. Navy as a training aircraft until 2003. (In 1962 the aircraft was redesignated A-4.)

## 9. F4H PHANTOM

The McDonnell F4H Phantom (first flight 1958) was one of the most successful fighter-attack aircraft of the Cold War and was produced in larger numbers than any other U.S. post-World War II aircraft except for the P-80/T-33 Shooting Star and F-86 Sabre/FJ Fury. The Phantom was flown by the U.S. Air Force and ten foreign air forces as well as from aircraft carriers by the U.S. Navy and Marine Corps, and the Royal Navy. In Vietnam the Phantom demonstrated that it was more than a match for the MiG-21s flown by North Vietnamese. Also employed as an attack aircraft, the U.S. Air Force variants were configured to deliver nuclear weapons. More than 5,000 Phantoms were produced. (In 1962 the Phantom was redesignated F-4.)

## 10. SEA HARRIER

The Hawker Siddeley Harrier (first flight 1966) was the world's first vertical/short take-off and landing (VSTOL) aircraft to enter military service. Its effectiveness was proven in the Falklands conflict of 1982, when Royal Navy Sea Harriers, operating from two small VSTOL carriers, inflicted major losses on Argentine aircraft. In that war both Navy and Royal Air Force ground-attack Harriers were also used in the strike role. The U.S. Marine Corps has flown Harriers from amphibious ships since 1971 (designated AV-8); variants are currently in service with British, Italian, and Spanish military services. McDonnell Douglas was the U.S. partner for AV-8 production.

# Most Unusual Aircraft to Fly from Carriers

## 1. POTEZ 56E

The first known operation of a multi-engine aircraft from an aircraft carrier took place in September 1936, when the single Potez 56E light transport operated aboard the French carrier *Béarn*. The twin-engine Potez 56E was the French Navy's adaptation of a six-passenger commercial aircraft, fitted with an arresting hook for shipboard trials. The French Navy also proposed modification of three twin-engine bombers for carrier operation—the Breguet Br. 693 (to be designated Br. 810), the SNCAO 600, and Dewoitine D.750. But these projects were not pursued.

## 2. B-25 MITCHELL

The North American B-25 Mitchell gained fame on April 18, 1942, when 16 of the medium bombers under Lt. Col. Jimmy Doolittle took off from the Navy carrier *Hornet* (CV 8) to attack several Japanese cities. But earlier, on February 2, 1942, two B-25s took off from the *Hornet* to demonstrate the feasibility of such an operation. Subsequently, on November 15, 1944, the Navy conducted takeoff and landing trials aboard the carrier *Shangri-La* (CV 38) with a PBJ-1H (Navy version of the B-25H). And, on April 21, 1972, two privately owned

Mitchells took off from the deck of the carrier *Ranger* (CVA 61) off San Diego in commemoration of the Doolittle flight.

### 3. **MOSQUITO**
The de Havilland Mosquito, a wooden, twin-engine aircraft, was one of the most versatile and effective combat aircraft of World War II. On March 25, 1944, Lt.-Comdr. Eric M. Brown made five landings and takeoffs on the British carrier *Indefatigable*. These trials led to the Royal Air Force establishing a Mosquito squadron for carrier operations, and the subsequent development of twin-engine Mosquito derivatives for Royal Navy carrier operations.

### 4. **VAMPIRE**
Lt.-Cmdr. Brown also receives credit for the first true jet landing aboard an aircraft carrier for when he landed a jet-propelled de Havilland Vampire I fighter aboard HMS *Ocean* on December 3, 1945. The Vampire was Britain's second jet-propelled combat aircraft. (On November 6, 1945, a U.S. Navy FR-1 composite piston-engine fighter piloted by Ens. Jake C. West lost power as he took off from the escort carrier *Wake Island* (CVE 65); West started his I-16 turbojet engine and immediately returned to the carrier to make a successful landing on jet power although it is believed his piston engine did not totally lose its power.)

### 5. **R4D SKYTRAIN**
The C-47 (Navy R4D) was the military version of the twin-engine Douglas DC-3, one of the most successful commercial transports ever produced. They were used extensively by U.S. and foreign military services during World War II and for decades afterward. On January 29, 1947, with Comdr. William M. Hawkes as pilot and Rear Adm. Richard E. Byrd as

co-pilot, the first of eight R4D aircraft took off from the carrier *Philippine Sea* (CV 47) and flew to the Little America base in Antarctica. A second R4D followed a few minutes later and four others were launched without incident the next day. As part of Operation Highjump, the six cargo planes provided U.S. Antarctic explorers with an unprecedented capability for exploration, aerial photography, and supply.

## 6. P2V NEPTUNE

The Lockheed P2V Neptune entered U.S. Navy service in 1947 and became the Navy's primary maritime reconnaissance/anti-submarine aircraft. More than a dozen other nations also flew the twin-engine bomber-type aircraft. When the Navy decided to develop an interim carrier-based nuclear strike capability, the Neptune was selected. Trial takeoffs from carriers of the *Midway* (CVB 41) class began on April 27, 1948, when Comdr. Thomas D. Davies took off from the carrier *Coral Sea* (CVB 43); a few minutes later a second Neptune took off. Afterwards the Navy acquired 12 P2V-3C variants specifically to deliver nuclear weapons. These aircraft made numerous takeoffs from the three *Midway*-class carriers, although no landings were attempted.

## 7. A3D SKYWARRIOR

The Douglas A3D Skywarrior was the largest aircraft to regularly operate from aircraft carriers. Designed as an all-weather nuclear strike aircraft, the twin-turbojet Skywarrior weighed more than 35 tons in carrier use, with tanker variants going to almost 40 tons. The Skywarrior entered service aboard carriers in the nuclear strike role in 1956; tanker, reconnaissance, and electronic warfare variants followed it. It was used in the Vietnam War as a conventional bomber as well as in several specialized roles. (In 1962 the Skywarrior was redesignated A-3.)

## 8. U-2 SPYPLANE

The Lockheed U-2 spyplane, developed in utmost secrecy, made 23 successful flights over the Soviet Union from 1956 to 1960. The aircraft was also flown over many other countries—some allied—to spy out secrets. The carrier flight tests of a U-2 occurred in August 1963, when Lockheed test pilot Bob Schumacher took off and made a number of practice approaches and then attempted—unsuccessfully—to land on the carrier *Kitty Hawk* (CVA 63). Afterwards, several U-2s were fitted with arresting hooks and successful trials were flown from several carriers. The only operational U-2 carrier mission—Operation Seeker—occurred in May 1964, when the *Ranger* (CVA 61) launched one or possibly two U-2G spyplanes to monitor the French nuclear tests at Murora Atoll in French Polynesia.

## 9. C-130 HERCULES

The Lockheed C-130 Hercules has been the most versatile and widely flown cargo aircraft developed since World War II. Used by the U.S. armed forces and numerous foreign services as well as commercial firms, the four-turboprop-engine C-130 is the largest aircraft to have flown from an aircraft carrier. A KC-130F conducted a series of carrier evaluation flights from the carrier *Forrestal* (CVA 59) in the fall of 1963. Lt. James H. Flatley III flew 16 in touch-and-go landings on October 30, 1963, and a week later he began full-stop landings as well as takeoffs from the ship. The maximum weight of the aircraft in the tests was 120,000 pounds.

## 10. XC-142 VSTOL

The first American-built vertical/short take-off and landing (VSTOL) aircraft to operate from a carrier was the Hiller-Ryan XC-142A, a tactical transport powered by four turboprop engines. The XC-142A had a tilt-wing that could rotate up to

100 degrees from the horizontal position to deflect its slip-stream, thus achieving vertical flight. During May 1966 an XC-142A made 50 landings and takeoffs aboard the carrier *Bennington* (CVS 20); 44 were short-run landings and six were in the vertical mode. The most dramatic maneuver was the aircraft making a vertical takeoff, hovering above the flight deck for a few moments, then changing wing angle, and speeding away in forward conventional flight. With a gross weight of about 30,000 pounds, the XC-142A had a speed range from 35 m.p.h. *backwards* to 400 m.p.h. in forward flight. In addition to the *Bennington*, the XC-142 also flew from a Navy amphibious ship. Five prototype XC-142 aircraft were produced; the aircraft was to carry 32 combat troops or 8,000 pounds of cargo.

# Rotary-Wing Aircraft

## 1. OP-1 AUTOGIRO

The Pitcairn OP-1 was the first rotary-wing aircraft to be flown by the U.S. Navy and Marine Corps. It obtained aerodynamic lift with a horizontal propeller—or rotor—that drew energy from the air stream rather than the aircraft's engine. Although the engine could be connected to the rotor during take-off or landing, in flight the engine was geared to a conventional propeller for forward motion. A speed of about 30 m.p.h. was needed to create an air flow over the rotor blades to maintain flight. Thus, the autogiro could take off and land vertically, but could not hover.

The Pitcairn autogiros were based on the design of Juan de la Cierva, a Spaniard who successfully flew a rotary-wing aircraft near Madrid in 1923; this was the progenitor for some 500 autogiros built in Western countries in the 1930s and early 1940s. (The Soviets developed their own line of autogiros.) The U.S. Navy, Marine Corps, and Army Air Corps evaluated the XOP-1 during the 1930s. The Navy acquired three XOP-1 autogiros in 1931, and one was tested aboard the pioneer aircraft carrier *Langley* (CV 1) on September 23, 1931. No further U.S. carrier operations were conducted with the autogiro. The following June one of the autogiros was sent to Nicaragua for use by the U.S. Marine Corps expeditionary force policing the guerrilla-infested mountain and jungle areas of that country. The aircraft could carry a pilot and observer.

## 2. **FL 282 HELICOPTER**

The Flettner Fl 282 was the world's first helicopter to be designed specifically for naval service and the world's first helicopter to enter military service. Based on Anton Flettner's earlier Fl 265, the Fl 282 had twin two-blade, intermeshing rotors (which alleviated the need for a tail rotor). The two-seat Fl 282 first flew in 1940. The German Navy took delivery of 29 prototypes of the Fl 282. In 1944 the Navy and Air Force placed orders for 1,000 helicopters. Mass production was begun, but Allied bombing soon halted the program. The prototypes were flown in the anti-submarine role from German ships in the Baltic, Aegean, and Mediterranean Seas. One landing on the deck of a surfaced submarine was reported. The single-engine helicopter weighted 2,205 pounds loaded, had a range of just over 100 miles with two crewmen (186 miles with one), and a maximum speed of 93 m.p.h.

## 3. **FA 330 AUTOMOTIVE KITE**

The Focke-Achgelis "automotive kite" was a unique rotary-wing aircraft towed by surfaced submarines. It was not self-propelled, although there were proposals to fit it with a small engine. The "helicopter" was intended to extend the visual range of the U-boat with the small, manned aircraft being put aloft in areas where enemy aircraft were not expected. Several U-boats did operate the Fa 330 during World War II, most if not all in the Indian Ocean. The aircraft had a steel tubular construction with a conventional tail assembly; it could be folded and dismantled for stowage in the submarine in a few minutes. The aircraft weighed 180 pounds empty and had a three-blade rotor diameter of 24 feet (increased to 28 feet in later aircraft). Launching the Fa 330 required a 17-m.p.h. airspeed, generated by the submarine speed plus the wind speed. Some 200 to 500 feet of steel cable were usually winched out for operation, with a telephone line being imbedded in the cable to enable the observer to communicate with the submarine. The free-wheeling rotor kept the craft aloft, with a normal altitude of about 330 feet. Cruising speed was up to 25 m.p.h. About 200 Fa 330s were produced.

### 4. R-4/HNS-1 HELICOPTERS

This was the first successful helicopter developed by Igor Sikorsky, who had first experimented with rotary-wing aircraft in Russia prior to World War I. Based on his VS-300 demonstration aircraft, the military R-4 was a two-seat helicopter that entered U.S. and British military service in World War II. The military XR-4 first flew in January 1942. It was the first U.S. rotary-wing aircraft to be mass-produced with 131 being built, including prototypes. The U.S. Navy variant, designated HNS-1, was operated by the Coast Guard (which was part of the Navy during the war). The U.S. Army flew tests with an XR-4 from a platform on the tanker *Bunker Hill* on May 6-7, 1943, and with the YR-4 from the Army transport *James Parker* on July 6-7, 1943. Subsequently, additional trials were flown aboard the British merchant ship *Daghestan* and the U.S. Coast Guard cutter *Cobb* (WPG 181). Navy HNS-1s subsequently flew from several types of ships pending the delivery of more advanced helicopters. The R-4/HNS-1 had a single, three-blade main rotor and a small tail rotor. The single-engine aircraft had a maximum speed of 75 m.p.h., and a range of 130 miles. The helicopter was fitted with wheels or floats, the latter permitting operations on land, water, and ice.

## 5. H-19/HO4S/HRS HELICOPTERS

The Sikorsky S 55 design was the first American helicopter to be certified for commercial operation and the first to be produced in four digit numbers for the U.S. armed forces. Known in the U.S. Navy and Coast Guard as the HO4S and in the U.S. Marine Corps as the HRS, the S-55 was flown as the H 19 by the U.S. Army and Air Force. It was also license built in other countries and after the HU-1/UH-1 Huey was probably the most widely flown helicopter in the West with some 40 nations operating military variants. The S 55 differed from most other helicopters in having the engine located in the nose, enabling the cabin to be placed at the center of gravity, thus allowing for considerable variations in payload without affecting aircraft stability; it also permitted easy access to the engine, which could be replaced in two hours. The cabin could accommodate up to ten troops, or six stretchers and two attendants, or 5,000 pounds of cargo. The first YH-19 prototype, ordered by the U.S. Air Force, flew in November 1949. The Navy accepted its first HO4S in August 1950, followed by the Coast Guard and Marine Corps (HRS variant). In the ASW role two pilots and a sonar operator manned the HO4S; it was fitted with AN/AQS-4 dipping sonar or carried one Mark 43 anti-submarine torpedo. The helicopters flew in pairs— one search and one attack helicopter. In the search mode (without a torpedo) its endurance was almost three hours. The Marine Corps, embracing the concept of vertical assault, bought 271 helicopters designated HRS, with the first delivered in April 1951. The HRS-1 was similar to the HO4S-1 but had troop seating and self-sealing fuel tanks. In the fall of 1951 a squadron of Marine-piloted HRS-2 helicopters was sent to Korea. These helicopters were used to lift supplies to isolated combat units, move reconnaissance and rocket units, evacuate wounded, and carry out vertical assault exercises. Occasionally the whirlybirds operated from the escort carriers in Korean waters, the harbinger of a new kind of carrier operation.

Several S 55s were transferred to Britain, where Westland soon began production, the British name being Whirlwind. The early Whirlwinds had piston engines, but these were soon changed to a turbine power plant, which provided some increase in performance, including reduced vibration, and had the important advantage of a quick startup. U.S. production was almost 1,300 helicopters with British, French, Japanese, and Yugoslav production bringing the total to more than 1,800. The basic H-19A had a radial engine that provided a maximum speed of 100 m.p.h., with a range of 400 miles.

## 6. DSN/QH-50 DASH HELICOPTERS

The Gyrodyne drone anti-submarine helicopter (DASH) was developed by the U.S. Navy for shipboard use to deliver anti-submarine weapons at greater distances than ship-launched weapons. It was also the only unmanned aircraft (i.e., intended for recovery) designed to carry a nuclear bomb. The British and Soviet Navies developed manned helicopters to exploit shipboard sonar detections; the U.S. Navy decided to develop an unmanned helicopter believing that a DASH could fly from smaller ships more easily than could a manned helicopter, operate in bad weather that would keep a manned helicopter on deck, and have a higher readiness. DASH was developed from the Gyrodyne firm's one-man "Rotorcycle," intended to carry a single Marine and his equipment. Gyrodyne's unmanned DSN-1 first flew in December 1958 and a DSN-1 made the first shipboard landing—with a pilot on board—on July 1, 1960, on the frigate *Mitscher* (DL 2). Following a dozen development aircraft, from 1960 to 1969 Gyrodyne produced 732 operational drones for the Navy plus one DSN-3 delivered to the Army. The definitive DSN-3 variant became operational in late 1962. The DASH fuselage had an aluminum tubular structure to which was attached the turboshaft engine, landing gear, and other equipment. Contra-rotating rotors alleviated the need for a tail boom and anti-torque tail rotor. It could carry one or two lightweight ASW torpedoes or a Mark 57 nuclear depth bomb. Maximum weight was 2,303 pounds; maximum speed was 92 miles per hour while the cruising speed was 63 miles per hour with an endurance of just over two hours. The effective radius of about 30 nautical miles was limited by the range of the ship's radar, required for the tracking and guidance of DASH. No sensors were carried by DASH. Drone availability lagged behind the availability of DASH-capable ships; for example, in December 1961 there were 41 ships but no operational DASHs; by mid-1964 there were 128 ships with 50 operational DASHs. In all, more than 200 warships were provided DASH facilities. Technical and, especially, operational problems plagued DASH, causing a large number of losses. The program ended in the U.S. Navy in January 1971. (The DSN designation was changed to QH 50 in 1962.)

### 7. HU-1/UH-1 HUEY HELICOPTERS

Officially named Iroquois, following the U.S. Army's scheme of naming helicopters for Indian tribes, this helicopter was developed by Bell as the XH-40 for battlefield use as a transport and casualty evacuation aircraft. It has been produced in greater numbers than any other helicopter—more than 16,000 built in several countries—and has been flown by about 60 nations. Several navies have flown specialized anti-submarine variants of the Huey. In the U.S. Navy it has been flown in the utility, training, rescue, and gunship roles; in the U.S. Marine Corps as a presidential transport and utility helicopter. The aircraft's first flight was in October 1956 and it entered U.S. Army service in 1958. Initially flown with one turboshaft engine, later variants have twin engines, with a distinctive, two-blade main rotor and a boom-supported tail rotor. The UH-1B could carry seven troops in addition to a three-man crew; top speed was 147 m.p.h. with a 380-mile range. Loaded weight was 8,500 pounds. ASW variants could carry dipping sonar and were armed with one or two lightweight ASW torpedoes. (The Huey—the name derived from its designation—was originally HU-1; changed in 1962 to UH-1.)

## 8. KA-25 HORMONE HELICOPTERS

The Kamov Ka-25 (NATO codename Hormone) was developed specifically for the Soviet Navy. The ship-based Hormone-A is an anti-submarine aircraft, the Hormone-B a missile-targeting helicopter, and the Hormone-C a utility and rescue variant. The Hormone-B was the world's only specialized "radar" helicopter until the British development of the Sea King helicopter with Searchwater radar in 1982. The Hormone-B is fitted with the larger Big Bulge-B radar for surface surveillance and can transmit targeting data via video data link to surface ships and submarines armed with anti-ship missiles. The Ka-25 has a distinctive configuration with a compact fuselage, two contra rotating rotors driven by twin turboshaft engines, and a short tail boom supporting a multi fin empennage: the rotor arrangement alleviates the need for a tail boom to facilitate shipboard handling. The main rotors also fold. The Hormone-A ASW configuration has the Puff-Ball surface search radar, expendable sonarbuoys, dipping sonar that can be lowered while the helicopter is hovering, and an internal weapons bay for ASW homing torpedoes or depth bombs. Hormone-C is a utility/passenger variant which can carry 12 passengers. (The helicopter is used as a civilian flying crane in the Ka-25K version.) The Hormone entered operational service in 1967. Powered by twin turboshaft engines, it has a loaded weight of 16,500 pounds, a maximum speed of 136 m.p.h., and a range of 300 miles.

## 9. H-53E SUPER STALLION/SEA DRAGON HELICOPTERS

The Sikorsky H-53E series helicopters, flown by the U.S. Marine Corps as the CH-53E Sea Stallion and by the Navy as the MH-53E Sea Dragon, is the largest helicopter of any navy to regularly operate from ships, both aircraft carriers and VSTOL/helicopter carriers. Developed specifically for the U.S. Navy and Marine Corps, the H-53E series is the heaviest lift helicopter in service outside of Russia. The first flight of the YCH-53E occurred in March 1974; and the CH-53E entered Marine Corps service in 1981. The CH-53E is flown by the Marines in the assault/heavy cargo roles and by the Navy in the vertical replenishment role, and by the Navy in the MH-53E mine countermeasures role. The H-53E can lift 16 tons of external load or carry 55 troops or small vehicles internally. The helicopter has three turboshaft engines driving a seven blade main rotor and tail rotor; in-flight refueling is provided. Gross takeoff weight is 73,500 pounds with a maximum speed of 195 m.p.h. at sea level and a range of 115 miles while carrying 16 tons of cargo. A more-capable CH-53K heavy-lift model is under development.

## 10. V-22 OSPREY TILT-ROTOR AIRCRAFT

The Bell-Boeing V-22 Osprey offers the first practical aircraft to combine the benefits of vertical flight with high-speed aircraft flight. The MV-22 troop version is flown by the U.S. Marine Corps with the Air Force flying the CV-22 variant as a special operations aircraft. The Navy had plans to procure the HV-22 for the search-and-rescue role, but procurement of that variant has been delayed indefinitely. Shipboard variants for anti-submarine warfare and airborne early warning have also been proposed. The V-22 design—developed from the Bell XV-15A technology-demonstration aircraft—has twin rotor turboshaft nacelles mounted on a connecting wing. The nacelles rotate to a horizontal position for conventional aircraft flight and are vertical for vertical take off and landing or hover. Conversion from the hovering mode to forward airplane flight takes 12 seconds. Rolling takeoffs and landings are the normal operating mode, although VTOL operations are feasible. Thus, the design has the advantages of both a conventional aircraft and helicopter. An in-flight refueling probe is provided. The basic aircraft has an internal cargo capacity of 20,000 pounds and an external (sling) capacity of 15,000 pounds. Thus, the MV-22 can internally carry 24 troops or nine litters, or a "Humvee" (high mobility multipurpose wheeled vehicle). Gross weight is some 54,000 pounds. Top speed is 316 m.p.h., with a range of 500 miles carrying 24 troops or 6,000 pounds of cargo.

# Airships, Blimps, and Balloons

Airships consist of rigid and non-rigid craft. Rigid airships have a rigid internal structure that contains the gas cells that provide lift for the craft; Zeppelins, named for their designer Count Ferdinand von Zeppelin, were such airships. A blimp contains no such structure, with the outer covering holding the gas cells. Spherical balloons containing lighter-than-air gas can be tethered (captive) or free.

## 1. THE FIRST BALLOONS

The first practical military balloon associated with "water" were those of American "balloonists." The Confederate balloonist John La Mountain made an ascent in a balloon from the deck of the small steamer *Fanny* while on the James River on August 3, 1861, to observe the countryside. A more ambitious undertaking began in 1861 when John A. Dahlgren, a Union Navy ordnance expert, modified the coal barge *George Washington Parke Custis* with a gas-generating apparatus developed by Thaddeus S.C. Lowe. On November 10, 1861, the steamer *Coeur de Lion* towed the barge from the Washington Navy Yard out into the Potomac River. The next day "aeronaut" Lowe inflated an observation balloon on the barge and, accompanied by Brig. Gen. Daniel E.

Sickles and others, ascended in the balloon while the barge was off Mattawomen Creek to observe Confederate forces three miles away in Virginia. These operations initiated the use of waterborne balloon observations.

## 2. THE FIRST AIRSHIPS
When World War I began in August 1914 the German Navy operated a single rigid airship (the German Army had six). The Navy saw the Zeppelin as an excellent reconnaissance platform for the fleet and soon acquired additional airships for that role. Beginning on January 19, 1915, naval airships began bombing raids over England and, on May 31, 1915, bombed London for the first time. These were the first "strategic" bombing operations against England. In a bombing raid against London on September 2, 1916, 12 naval airships and four Army airships bombed the city. Throughout 1915 the naval Zeppelins raided the Allied capitals of London and Paris with relative safety, but by the fall of 1916 the hydrogen-filled Zeppelins were becoming highly vulnerable to opposing fighter aircraft. Soon German Army bombers replaced the increasingly vulnerable "Zeps" in strategic raids. Fregattenkapitän Peter Strasser commanded the German Navy's Zeppelin force in World War I. Having joined the Navy at age 15, he personally led Zeppelin raids on Britain. Strasser died when the Z.70 was shot down over the Norfolk coast on August 6, 1918.

## 3. FIRST U.S. navy AIRSHIP
The U.S. Navy's first airship was the DN-1, the designation indicating Dirigible Navy No. 1. Built in 1916 by the Connecticut Aircraft Company, the airship had two engines with swiveling propellers that were to assist in vertical flight; its control car or gondola was shaped like a boat to allow it to

alight on the water. The *DN-1* was overweight and one of its engines had to be removed. The airship operated from a floating hangar at Pensacola, Florida. It made three flights in April 1917, after which it was scrapped.

## 4. FLYING AIRCRAFT CARRIERS

The U.S. Navy built and acquired from overseas five rigid airships beginning in 1923. The most notable Navy rigids were the flying aircraft carriers *Akron* and *Macon*. These 785-foot airships were commissioned in 1931 and 1933, respectively. Each airship could carry four Curtiss F9C-2 Sparrowhawk biplane fighters, which they could launch and recover while in flight. Their gas volume was 6,500,000 cubic feet of non-explosive helium. These airships were to scout ahead of the fleet, with the fighters to fend off enemy attackers. Their range was rated at 9,200 miles. The *Akron* crashed at sea in April 1933, as did the *Macon* in February 1935. These losses ended the Navy's rigid airship program. Besides having names, the rigids were in commission and on the Navy List, the same as surface ships and submarines.

## 5. THE METAL AIRSHIP

The U.S. Navy's *ZMC-2*, built by the Aircraft Development Corporation between 1926 and 1929, was highly unusual in that it had a thin metal skin in place of the fabric skin of all other airships. The designation indicated Metal Clad, with Z being the Navy's symbol for lighter-than-air craft. The *ZMC-2* flew for a decade without significant problems. Its envelope held 22,600 cubic feet of helium, and it was 149½ feet long.

## 6. WARTIME BLIMPS

The U.S. Navy began World War II in December 1941 with seven operational blimps. During the war a large number were procured for maritime patrol/anti-submarine operations, most of the K-class. When the conflict ended in August 1945, the Navy had 168 blimps, which had flown 55,900 operational flights for a total of 550,000 flight hours. The airships escorted many convoys and flew independent patrols. They sank no U-boats and one, the *K-74*, was shot down by the submarine *U-134* in the Florida Straits on July 18, 1943. (The U-boat was attacked and damaged by a U.S. aircraft on July 19, and sunk off the coast of Spain when an RAF bomber attacked it on August 24. All 48 men on board were lost.)

The K-series had envelopes of up to 456,000 cubic feet with a length up to 253 feet. They had twin engines and normally carried a crew of nine. Their armament was several machine guns and a few depth charges. Cruising speed was 50 knots with a maximum speed rated at 67.5 knots.

## 7. THE MYSTERY BLIMP

The U.S. Navy's *L-8* was involved in one of the most bizarre mysteries of all time. On August 16, 1942, the blimp departed Treasure Island in San Francisco Bay with a crew of two on a routine patrol off the coast. The airship later drifted across the coastline and crashed in Dale City. There was no one on board; both Navy officers had disappeared. There was no pre-crash damage to the blimp and no distress call had been transmitted by its radio. Most likely the crew had hovered close to the water to retrieve a piece of wreckage or debris. One man had leaned out too far and fell into the water; the second, trying to assist him, suffered the same fate.

## 8. AIRBORNE EARLY WARNING BLIMPS

After World War II the U.S. Navy developed a series of blimps for the airborne early warning (AEW) role, to provide over-ocean surveillance to detect Soviet bombers approaching the United States. The first of these was the Goodyear-built *ZPG-2W* series, with the first of five such blimps completed in May

1955. The *ZPG-2W* had a 975,000-cubic-foot envelope with a length of 342½ feet. A large air search radar antenna was fitted beneath the control car and a height-finding radar was mounted within the envelope with a small radome protruding from the top of the blimp.

## 9. THE LONGEST FLIGHT

The *ZPG-2* blimp named *Snow Bird* lifted off from the Naval Air Station South Weymouth, Massachusetts, on the evening of March 4, 1957, under the command of Comdr. Jack R. Hunt with 13 crew members. On March 13 the *Snow Bird* broke the record for continuous non-refueled flight, which was 200 hours, 12 minutes, and later that day surpassed the distance record for non-refueled flight established by the German airship *Graf Zeppelin* in 1929 of 6,980 miles. The *Snow Bird*, traveled from the U.S. east coast across the Atlantic to North Africa, and then back across the Atlantic toward Puerto Rico. The airship landed at Key West, Florida, on the evening of March 15, 1957, having been aloft for 264.2 hours while flying 9,448 miles.

## 10. THE LARGEST BLIMP

The largest blimp ever built was the U.S. Navy's *ZPG-3W*, the last operational lighter-than-air craft built for the U.S. Navy before the blimp program ended in August 1962. Built by Goodyear, the *ZPG-3W* had a 40-foot air search radar antenna installed within its 1,516,000-cubic-foot envelope. The craft was 403¼ feet long; with a crew of about 25, the blimp could reach 94 m.p.h., although its cruising speed was 52 m.p.h. The *ZPG-3W* made her first flight in July 1958. A total of four AEW-configured airships of this design were produced for the Navy through 1960. These were the last of 241 non-rigid airships flown by the U.S. Navy from 1917 to 1962.

# Submarine Firsts

### 1. ATTACK ON AN ENEMY SHIP

The first "submarine" attack on an enemy ship occurred on the night of September 7, 1776, when the submersible *Turtle,* devised by Connecticut inventor David Bushnell, attacked HMS *Eagle* in New York Harbor. The craft's operator, Sgt. Ezra Lee, a volunteer soldier, attempted to drill into the British ship's keel to attach a powder charge. The attempt was foiled by the *Eagle*'s copper-sheathed hull. The gunpowder charge exploded harmlessly and the *Turtle* escaped.

In the War of 1812, Bushnell built a similar submersible that attacked HMS *Ramillies* at anchor off New London, Connecticut. This attempt also failed although the craft's operator successfully bored a hole in the ship's copper sheathing.

### 2. COMMISSIONED SUBMARINE

The first submarine to be formally commissioned in a navy was the USS *Holland* (SS 1), designed and built by Irish immigrant schoolteacher John P. Holland. Holland built his first submarine in 1875, but the Navy rejected it and several others. His 1898 submarine was placed in commission in 1900 as the USS *Holland*. The craft was propelled on the surface by a gasoline engine and submerged by an electric motor powered by batteries. The 53⁵⁄₆-foot craft was armed with one 18-inch torpedo tube (three torpedoes) and a pneumatic dynamite gun that fired through the bow. Britain, Japan, and other countries subsequently procured Holland's submarines.

### 3. SINKING AN ENEMY WARSHIP UNDERWAY

The ill-fated Confederate *H.L. Hunley* was the first submarine to sink an enemy ship—the anchored Union warship *Housatonic*. The German submarine *U-21* under Kapitän-leutnant Otto Hersing sank the British light cruiser *Pathfinder* in the North Sea on September 5, 1914—the first submarine to sink an enemy warship that was underway. The *Pathfinder* went down with 259 of her crew of 296.

### 4. CARGO SUBMARINE

The world's first—and so far only operational—civilian cargo submarine was the German *Deutschland*, completed in 1916 to carry cargo between Germany and the United States during World War I. The largest submarine yet built in Germany, she had an 800-ton cargo capacity on a surface displacement of 1,440 tons; of that cargo, some 250 tons of rubber were to be carried in floodable compartments external to the pressure hull. She was unarmed. Under Capt. Paul König, a veteran merchant marine officer, the *Deutschland* made two voyages to the United States, on both occasions evading British warships blockading Germany and specifically hunting for the cargo submarine. Subsequently, the *Deutschland*, as the *U-155*—and several similar submarines—were armed and served in the German Navy.

### 5. BATTLESHIP SUNK BY A SUBMARINE

The first capital warship to be sunk by an undersea craft was the Turkish battleship *Messudiyeh*, torpedoed and sunk by the British submarine *B11* in the Dardanelles on December 13, 1914. However, the *Messudiyeh*, completed in 1874, displacing some 10,000 tons and 331 feet long, barely ranked among the world's battleships in 1914.

More significant, the British battleship *Formidable*, a 15,000-ton, 430-foot warship completed in 1898, was sunk by the German *U-24* off Portland Bill on January 1, 1915. Commanded by Kapitänleutnant Rudolf Schneider, the *U-24* fired a single torpedo that stopped the battleship; 45 minutes later Schneider fired a second, which sank the warship. There were only 233 survivors from the 780-man crew of the *Formidable*.

## 6. NUCLEAR SUBMARINE

The USS *Nautilus* (SSN 571) was the world's first nuclear-propelled vehicle. Built by the Electric Boat Company in Groton, Connecticut, she was completed in early 1955. The *Nautilus* was a combat submarine, the 320-foot, 3,532-ton submarine being armed with six bow torpedo tubes. Under her first commanding officer, Comdr. Eugene P. Wilkinson, the *Nautilus* demonstrated unprecedented underwater performance. During her 24 years in commission the *Nautilus* nuclear plant was refueled three times; on her four nuclear cores she sailed:

| | |
|---|---|
| 1955–1957 | 62,559.6 n.miles of which 36,498 n.miles were submerged |
| 1957–1959 | 91,325 n.miles |
| 1959–1967 | 174,507 n.miles |
| 1967–1979 | 162,382 n.miles |

The *Nautilus* was in active Navy service as both a laboratory and an operational combat submarine until 1979. She is preserved as a museum at New London, Connecticut.

The USS *Nautilus* (SSN 571)—the world's first nuclear-propelled ship—loads a torpedo. *U.S. Navy*

## 7. LAUNCHING A BALLISTIC MISSILE

The first submarine to launch a ballistic missile—a strategic weapon that, with a nuclear warhead, could threaten an enemy's homeland—was the Soviet submarine *B-67* (modified NATO codename Zulu). On September 16, 1955, in the White Sea, the submarine launched an R-11FM ballistic missile that streaked 135 nautical miles to impact in the remote Novaya Zemlya test range. Several diesel-electric submarines of this type were employed in the early Soviet ballistic missile program. The first launch of a ballistic missile from a nuclear submarine was a Polaris A-1 missile from the USS *George Washington* (SSBN 598) on June 20, 1960.

## 8. REACHING THE NORTH POLE

On August 3, 1958, the nuclear-propelled submarine *Nautilus* crossed the North Pole during a submerged transit from the Bering Strait (between Alaska and Siberia) to the Greenland Sea. Commanded at the time by Comdr. William R. Anderson, there were 116 men aboard the *Nautilus* during the submerged transit of 1,830 nautical miles.

## 9. SURFACING AT THE NORTH POLE

Although the *Nautilus* was the first submarine to reach the North Pole, the nuclear submarine *Skate* (SSN 578), completed in late 1957, was the first submarine ever to surface at the geographic North Pole. Under Comdr. James F. Calvert, the *Skate* reached the pole on the evening of March 11, 1958. Soon thereafter she surfaced some 40 miles from the pole. The submarine continued operations near the pole for several days with several surfacings through the ice; in all she spent 10 days, 14 hours under the ice while traveling 2,405 nautical miles.

## 10. AROUND THE WORLD SUBMERGED

The first submerged transit around the world was made by the nuclear-propelled submarine *Triton* (SSRN 586), commanded by naval officer-author Edward L. ("Ned") Beach. Completed in November 1959, the radar picket submarine was the world's largest at the time, with an overall length of 447½ feet. On February 16, 1960, she submerged off Long Island, New York, and roughly followed the path of Fredinand Magellan's circumnavigation of 1519. Twice during the cruise the *Triton* partially broke the surface, once to disembark an ill sailor, and once to embark two officers and disembark another. The submarine surfaced off the Delaware coast on May 10 after a submerged transit of 60 days, 21 hours that covered 26,723 nautical miles.

# Submarine Records

### 1. LARGEST SUBMARINE GUN
Submarines in the pre-nuclear propulsion era, being limited in underwater endurance, usually were fitted with deck guns for attacking surface targets, generally merchant ships. The largest deck gun mounted for that purpose was 8-inches in diameter, with the French submarine cruiser *Surcouf* (completed in 1934) mounting two 8-inch weapons.

The largest gun ever fitted in a submarine, however, was a 12-inch gun for shore bombardment that was mounted in the British submarine monitors *M1, M2,* and *M3* (first completed in 1918).

### 2. LARGEST DIESEL-ELECTRIC SUBMARINE
The largest non-nuclear submarine to be built was the Japanese *I-400*, the lead ships of a class of aircraft-carrying submarines. She was completed in December 1944 at the Kure Navy Yard. She displaced 3,530 tons standard and was 400¼ feet long. The *I-400s* could carry three floatplanes, launched from a catapult track in the forward deck.

### 3. SMALLEST SUBMARINE
Several navies have built and operated small or "midget" submarines—Britain, Germany, Italy, Japan, and the United States.

Probably the smallest such craft that had the basic features of a true submarine were the German Type XXVIIA *Hecht* midget submarines. These 11¾-ton, 34-foot craft had a crew of two. The *Hecht* could carry a single mine or a torpedo slung under the hull with a 90-mile radius of action. Almost 200 of these craft were planned but only a few were completed in 1944–1945.

## 4. FASTEST DIESEL-ELECTRIC SUBMARINE

The U.S. research submarine *Albacore* (AGSS 569)—built to test advanced, high-speed submarine features—was completed at the Portsmouth (Maine) Naval Shipyard in 1953. The *Albacore* introduced the advanced "tear-drop" hull configuration and, during her 18 years of service, she tested speed brakes, a parachute slow-down system, contra-rotating propellers, "X" tail fins, polymers, and other features. During her career, the submarine reached a submerged speed of 37 knots.

## 5. DEEPEST DIVING UNDERWATER VEHICLE

Bathyscaphs are distinguished from submarines by having limited horizontal mobility, being essentially an underwater "elevator." The U.S. Navy's bathyscaph *Trieste* on January 23, 1960, reached the deepest known ocean depth—35,800 feet in the Challenger Deep off Guam. Designed and built by Augustus Piccard, the craft was purchased by the U.S. Navy for deep-ocean research in 1958. She was piloted by Navy Lt. Don Walsh, with Piccard's son Jacques on board, when she reached the record depth. After major modifications, the *Trieste* continued in service and dived on the wreckage of the U.S. nuclear submarines *Thresher* (SSN 593) and *Scorpion* (SSN 589).

## 6. DEEPEST-DIVING DIESEL-ELECTRIC SUBMARINE

The deepest-diving U.S. submarine was the diesel-electric research submarine *Dolphin* (AGSS 555), completed in 1968. She had an operating depth of about 3,000 feet.

## 7. FASTEST NUCLEAR-PROPELLED SUBMARINE

The Soviet nuclear-propelled cruise missile submarine *K-162* (NATO codename Papa), completed in December 1969, was the world's fastest submarine. In 1970 she achieved a speed of 44.7 knots. The *K-162* was constructed of titanium.

The fastest U.S. nuclear-propelled submarine is believed to be the USS *Seawolf* (SSN 21), completed in 1997. The U.S. Chief of Naval Operations, Adm. James Watkins, publicly revealed that the submarine had a design speed of 35 knots.

## 8. LARGEST NUCLEAR-PROPELLED SUBMARINE

The largest nuclear-propelled submarines were the six ships of the Soviet Akula class (NATO codename Typhoon). These are giant, ballistic missile submarines. The lead submarine, the *TK-208*, was completed in 1981 at the Severdovnsk shipyard. These submarines had a surface displacement of 23,200 tons and were 564 feet long. Each submarine carried 20 large, underwater-launch ballistic missiles in addition to torpedoes.

The largest U.S. undersea craft are the 18 Trident ballistic missile submarines, led by the USS *Ohio* (SSBN 726), commissioned in 1981. She displaces 16,764 tons surfaced and is 560 feet long.

## 9. DEEPEST-DIVING NUCLEAR-PROPELLED SUBMARINE

The Soviet submarine *Komsomolets* (NATO codename Mike) was the world's deepest diving nuclear-propelled submarine.

A torpedo attack submarine, the *Komsomolets*, completed in 1984, had an operating depth in excess of 3,300 feet.

## 10. MOST HEAVILY ARMED MISSILE SUBMARINE

The U.S. Trident submarines of the *Ohio* (SSBN 726) class carry 24 Trident ballistic missiles, each of which carries a multiple warhead of eight nuclear warheads that can be aimed at separate targets. Fourteen of these submarines were completed beginning in 1984.

The most heavily armed submarines with conventional missiles are the four *Ohio*-class submarines that were converted to combination cruise missile-troop carrying submarines (SSGN). These submarines can carry up to 154 Tomahawk land-attack cruise missiles with conventional warheads.

# Submarine Disasters

## 1. FIRST SUBMARINE ESCAPE

Submarine *escape* is the means by which sailors in a submarine escape without outside help, the latter being termed *rescue*. The first escape occurred on February 1, 1851, from the submarine *Le Plongeur Martin*, constructed by Wilhelm Bauer, in the Bavarian artillery. His submarine, constructed of iron plates and powered by a hand-wheel-operated propeller, sank in trials off Kiel, Germany, in 60 feet of water. Bauer and his two assistants waited until the craft was almost completely flooded, opened the hatch, and swam to the surface. They were unharmed after being submerged for five hours.

## 2. FIRST MILITARY SUBMARINE LOSS

The first military submarine to be lost was the *H. L. Hunley*, built in the Confederate States to attack Union warships during the American Civil War. A modified iron boiler almost 40 feet long, it was propelled by men turning cranks to turn a propeller to produce a speed of four knots. The craft towed a "torpedo" with 90 pounds of gunpowder on a 200-foot line that was to be dragged against an enemy ship. The *Hunley* sank two or three times during trials, with the loss of most of the men on board, including H. L. Hunley, who financed the project. Finally, on the night of February 17, 1864, armed with a spar torpedo, the *Hunley* rammed and sank the anchored Union warship *Housatonic*—and sank again with all hands.

### 3. FIRST SUBMARINE RESCUE

The U.S. submarine *Squalus* (SS 192), completed in 1939, sank through accidental flooding on May 23, 1939, off Portsmouth, New Hampshire, with the loss of 26 crewmen. Thirty-three other men were trapped in the boat at a depth of 243 feet. In the first—and to date only—use of a rescue device to save submarine survivors, the Navy's McCann rescue chamber, lowered by cable from the USS *Falcon* (ASR 2), made four trips to rescue all of the trapped men. Navy divers, in attaching the cable for the McCann chamber to the submarine, made some of the most difficult open-sea dives ever accomplished. The *Squalus* was salvaged and returned to service as the USS *Sailfish* and served in World War II.

### 4. FIRST NUCLEAR SUBMARINE LOSS

The USS *Thresher* (SSN 593) was the world's first nuclear submarine to be lost. She sank during post-overhaul trials off the New England coast in 8,400 feet of water on April 10, 1963, taking with her all 129 men on board—112 Navymen and 17 civilian Navy employees. The cause of her loss was probably a reactor "scram" (shutdown) coupled with the failure of the submarine's ballast blowing system and the auxiliary electric propulsion system. The *Thresher* disaster remains history's worst submarine disaster in terms of lives lost.

### 5. MOST UNUSUAL LOSS

In some respects the most unusual submarine loss was that of the Israeli submarine *Dakar*, which disappeared just after midnight on January 25, 1968, with all 69 men on board, while en route from Britain to Israel. The former British submarine *Totem*, she had last reported by radio that morning when she was 360 nautical miles west of the coast of Israel (between Crete and Cyprus). The submarine's tethered rescue buoy—with the cable broken—was later found on the coast of Sinai. For more than 31 years the Israelis searched for the *Dakar*'s remains, a search that included the U.S. nuclear submersible *NR-1*. The missing submarine was found on May 28, 1999, based on analytical studies by Israeli and U.S. specialists. Damage to the *Dakar*'s sail structure—now in the Haifa naval museum—indicated that the submarine was sunk by collision with a merchant ship.

### 6. FIRST NUCLEAR WEAPONS LOSS
The second nuclear submarine to be lost, the USS *Scorpion* (SSN 589), was the first to sink with nuclear weapons on board. Returning from a deployment to the Mediterranean, the submarine sank with all hands—99 officers and enlisted men—on May 22, 1968, 400 nautical miles southwest of the Azores. While the exact cause has never been established, the most likely reason for her loss was a problem with her propeller shaft, which permitted rapid flooding of the submarine. At the time she carried two Mark 45 ASTOR (anti-submarine torpedo) weapons with nuclear warheads.

### 7. FIRST SOVIET NUCLEAR SUBMARINE LOSS
The first Soviet nuclear submarine to be lost, and the third following the USS *Thresher* and USS *Scorpion*, was the *K-8* (NATO codename November class). On April 11, 1970, as Soviet naval forces were conducting a multi-ocean exercise known as Okean (Ocean), the submarine *K-8* suffered an engineering casualty and fire while operating submerged in

the Atlantic, off Cape Finisterre, Spain. The submarine was able to reach the surface and efforts were made to save the craft. However, the submarine plunged into the depths on April 12. Other Soviet ships saved some of her crew, but 52 men were lost.

## 8. MOST NUCLEAR WEAPONS LOSS
The Soviet ballistic missile submarine *K-219* (NATO codename Yankee class) sank after a missile tube fire devastated the submarine some 600 nautical miles east of Bermuda on October 6, 1986. The submarine was able to surface and there was only one fatality among the crew of approximately 120 men. When the submarine sank she was carrying 15 RSM-25 (NATO designation SS-N-6) ballistic missiles with nuclear warheads and probably two torpedoes with nuclear warheads.

## 9. DEEPEST SUBMARINE ESCAPE
The deepest submarine escape occurred on April 7, 1989, when the Soviet nuclear-propelled submarine *Komsomolets* (NATO codename Mike class) sank off the coast of Norway in some 5,500 feet of water. After severe fires erupted in the submarine, the commanding officer, Capt. 1/Rank Yevgeniy Alekseyevich Vanin, was able to bring the submarine to the surface, where most of the crew were able to get off into rafts, although many died in the water of hypothermia, heart failure, or drowning. Suddenly the submarine plunged into the depths. As the submarine went down, Vanin and four other men entered an escape chamber; the chamber was ejected from the *Komsomolets* as she struck the ocean floor. The chamber reached the surface, but because of toxic gases in the chamber only two men survived; Vanin died. This was the first known use of a submarine escape chamber in an actual emergency situation.

## 10. LARGEST NUCLEAR SUBMARINE LOSS

The Soviet submarine *Kursk* (NATO codename Oscar class) that sank in the Barents Sea on August 12, 2000, with the loss of all on board, was the largest submarine ever sunk. The 472$^1$/$_3$-foot submarine had a surface displacement of 13,500 tons. She was sunk by an internal weapons explosion in her torpedo room that sent the *Kursk* to the bottom in some 350 feet of water. Twenty-three of the 118 men on board survived for several days in an after compartment, but could not be rescued. The *Kursk* was later raised and scrapped.

# Guns

Early naval guns were measured by the weight of their projectile or ball, in pounds (e.g., 32-pounder). Today large guns are measured by their inner barrel diameter, which is measured in inches or millimeters for larger guns and millimeters (mm) for smaller weapons. Guns less than one inch in diameter are also measured in "calibers," as .30 caliber (i.e., 3/10ths of an inch in diameter). The length of the gun's bore is expressed in multiples of its diameter; thus, a 76-mm/62-caliber gun has a bore or inner barrel length of 4,712 mm or approximately 185½ inches (4.7 m).

## 1. 18.1-INCH (460-MM) BATTLESHIP GUNS

The largest guns ever mounted by a warship were the 18.1-inch/45-caliber guns of the Japanese super battleship *Yamato* (completed 1941) and her sister ship *Musashi* (1942). The two ships, with a standard displacement of 62,000 tons, each carried nine 18.1-inch guns in three turrets. Twenty-seven 18.1-inch guns were produced, with nine intended for the similar *Shinano*, which was instead completed as an aircraft carrier. The guns had a maximum range of just under 46,000 yards and could fire an armor-piercing shell weighing 3,220 pounds. Their rate of fire was 1.5 rounds per minute per barrel.

## 2. 18-INCH (457-MM) CRUISER GUN

Only one warship ever mounted an 18-inch gun, HMS *Furious*, begun as a "large light cruiser" in 1915. She was designed to mount two 18-inch guns, in single-gun turrets forward and aft. (Two near sister ships, the *Courageous* and *Glorious* were built with 15-inch guns.) During her construction, the *Furious* was modified with a 228-foot aircraft flying-off deck and hangar forward, retaining the after 18-inch gun. She joined the fleet in July 1917, and after limited flight operations, in 1917–1918 she was modified with the after 18-inch gun being replaced by a land-on deck. Subsequently, the *Furious*, which served through World War II, was given a full-deck configuration. The 18-inch gun fired a 3,600-pound shell. Two spare 18-inch guns were fitted in the monitors *Lord Clive* and *General Wolff.*

## 3. 16-INCH BATTLESHIP GUNS

The Mark 7 16-inch/50-caliber gun was the largest gun fitted in U.S. warships. The weapon was fitted in the four battleships of the *Iowa* (BB 61) class (completed 1943–1944) and were planned for the five never-built *Montana* (BB 67) class. Each ship was designed to mount nine guns in triple turrets. (Two additional *Iowa*-class battleships were not completed.) Their maximum range was 40,185 yards firing a 2,700-pound armor-piercing projectile. The rate of fire was two rounds per minute per barrel. A nuclear projectile with a W23 warhead was available for these guns from December 1956 to October 1962.

## 4. 8-INCH (240-MM) DESTROYER GUN

The Mark 71 8-inch/55-caliber gun was developed specifically as a lightweight weapon for U.S. destroyer-size ships. Known as the major caliber lightweight gun (MCLWG), the weapon was planned for installation in some or all of the 31 destroyers of the *Spruance* (DD 963) class for the shore-bombardment role. But only one MCLWG went to sea, in the destroyer *Hull* (DD 945), which carried out highly successful trials from 1975 to 1979. However, the Secretary of Defense cancelled the program in 1978. The gun's range was 31,400 yards with a rate of fire of 12 rounds per minute or six guided projectiles per minute. The standard projectile weighed 260 pounds.

### 5. 6.1-INCH (155-MM) ADVANCED GUN SYSTEM

The advanced gun system (AGS) is the longest-range gun ever developed for warship use, having an estimated range in excess of 85 nautical miles. The gun was developed specifically for destroyers to use against land targets. It is planned for the highly controversial *Zumwalt* (DDG 1000) design, with the first ship to be delivered in 2014. Each ship will have two AGS mounts. The gun will fire the rocket-boosted long-range land attack projectile (LRLAP) at the rate of 12 rounds per minute with the rounds guided by external targeting means. Projectiles will weigh up to 225 pounds carrying a 24-pound explosive warhead.

### 6. 2-POUNDER (40-MM) POM-POM

"Pom-pom" was slang for the highly effective British close-in anti-aircraft gun mounting. Officially rated as a 2-pounder, the pom-pom came in single and quad mounts for smaller ships and 8-barrel mounts for battleships, large cruisers, and aircraft carriers. Single and twin mounts were also used ashore. Developed in World War I and first evaluated at sea in the early 1920s, the pom-pom by the 1930s was fitted in numerous British warships. By the end of World War II there were up to eight 8-barrel pom-pom mountings in the *King George V*-class battleships and six 8-barrel guns in the *Illustrious*-class carriers. Smaller warships generally had a four- and single-barrel mountings. Each barrel had a rate of fire of approximately 100 rounds per minute. The belted ammunition was fed from 114- or 140-round loading trays. The gun had a maximum range of 6,800 yards and a ceiling of 13,000 feet (falling between the 40-mm Bofors and 20-mm Oerlikon guns). Each round weighed just under two pounds.

## 7. **40-MM BOFORS**

The Swedish-design, rapid-fire 40-mm Bofors was the most widely used anti-aircraft gun of World War II. First produced in 1930, it was in the arsenal of most Allied and Axis nations, and in all theaters of the war. The U.S. Army had a large number of them and they were the U.S. Navy's most widely used gun aboard ship. In their report on anti-aircraft guns, military writers Peter Chamberlain and Terry Gander concisely described the Bofors in their *Anti-Aircraft Guns* (1975): "It was reliable, efficient and available, and gunners on both sides could ask no more of any gun." Shipboard 40-mm Bofors had a cyclic rate of 160 rounds-per-minute; however, because it was manually loaded, a 60 to 90 rounds-per-minute rate more was realistic. The Bofors were fitted in single, twin, and quad mounts.

## 8. **20-MM OERLIKON**

This Swiss-design rapid-fire, anti-aircraft gun was also extensively used by Allied and Axis navies during the war. The gun had established a favorable reputation in the Spanish Civil War and it was adopted by the Japanese Navy, which made several improvements (although few guns were procured). Subsequently, the British adopted it for merchant ships, which influenced the U.S. Navy's decision to begin installing it in warships in late 1941. The 20-mm weapon was produced by several nations in single, twin, and triple mounts.

## 9. 20-MM PHALANX CLOSE-IN WEAPON SYSTEMS

The 20-mm/76-caliber Phalanx close-in weapon system (CIWS) was developed as a terminal defense against attacking cruise missiles. The installation of Phalanx CIWS in U.S. warships followed by several years the appearance of similar rapid-fire gun systems, of larger caliber, in Soviet surface warships. The system is designated both Mark 15 and Mark 16 by the U.S. Navy, with the 20 mm gun subsystem designated Mark 26. The Phalanx underwent initial at-sea tests in 1973 with production mounts first installed in the aircraft carrier *Coral Sea* (CVA 43) in 1980. Developed from the aircraft-mounted M61A1 Vulcan rotary gun system, the Phalanx is a totally integrated weapon system that includes the AN/VPS-2 Ku-band search and track radar, gun, magazine, weapon control unit, and associated electronics, all fitted into a single unit 15 feet high and weighing about six tons. Thus, it is suitable for small combat craft as well as larger warships with one to four mounts being installed in various size ships. Maximum range is 1,625 yards with a theoretical firing rate of 3,000 rounds per minute, a very low dispersion rate, and initially a 989-round magazine; updated guns have a 1,550-round magazine. The projectile weight is 0.22 pounds. The Phalanx CIWS is fitted in warships of several other nations.

## 10. .50-CALIBER (12.7-MM) M2 MACHINE GUN

The M2 .50-caliber machine gun was probably produced in greater numbers, was in service longer, and is used by more nations than any other heavy machine gun. John Moses Browning (1855–1926) was one of America's most prolific gun inventors. After making his first gun from scrap metal at the age of 13, he went on to design pistols, rifles, and machine guns. His M2 heavy machine gun was designed toward the end of World War I and began its U.S. Army service in

1921. It was soon fitted on U.S. Navy warships for the anti-aircraft role and on small craft, motor torpedo boats, and landing craft. It was also installed in a variety of military aircraft. It remains in U.S. military service, today having also been adopted by numerous foreign military forces. The M2 weighs about 85 pounds, has an effective range of some 3,000 yards, and a rate of fire of more than 120 rounds per minute. Twin and quad mounts have been developed. All M2s are recoil-operated weapons firing belt-fed ammunition (initially fabric and later metal-link belts that disintegrate as the rounds are fired).

# Torpedoes

## 1. THE FIRST

The first successful self-propelled ("automobile") torpedo was developed by Robert Whitehead, an Englishman and highly respected engineer. In 1856 he joined an Italian marine engineering firm and soon turned his talents to designing a torpedo. With Giovanni Luppis, a retired Austrian naval officer, Whitehead developed his first torpedo in 1857. It was 11 feet long, 14 inches in diameter, weighed 300 pounds and had a speed of about six knots carrying 18 pounds of dynamite. They soon sold torpedoes to the Austrian Navy and, subsequently, to several other navies. The Luppis-Whitehead "fish" could be launched from tubes on the deck of surface ships or from underwater tubes in ships and submarines. In 1877 the first Whitehead torpedo launched in action was fired by the British cruiser *Shah* in her fight with the Peruvian monitor *Huscar*. The attack failed, as did the first attempt to use the Whitehead torpedoes by the Russians in their war with Turkey the same year. On January 26, 1878, however, the Russian torpedo boats *Chesma* and *Sinop* off Batoum attacked and sank a Turkish steamer—the first ship known to have been sunk by a self-propelled torpedo.

## 2. GNAT

Known by the Allies as the German naval acoustic torpedo, the GNAT was the world's first operational acoustic homing torpedo. It was used by U-boats against Allied anti-submarine ships in World War II. The acoustic-homing torpedo, called Zaunkönig (wren) and designated T5 by the German Navy, had acoustic guidance to search out the cavitation noises made by a surface ship's propellers. The first use of the GNAT was on September 20, 1943, when U-boats attacking convoy ON.202 damaged a frigate with an acoustic torpedo, requiring the ship to be taken in tow. In three days the GNATs were used to sink a destroyer, frigate, and corvette, and caused major damage to two other escort ships. The three-day action involved two adjacent convoys with a total of 69 merchant ships, which were attacked by 21 U-boats; six merchant ships and three U-boats were sunk in the action. The British had learned of GNAT prior to its use through prisoner of war interrogations and codebreaking. Forewarned, the British quickly developed the Foxer devices to decoy the torpedoes away from warships. These were put into service only 18 days after the convoy action described above. The Foxers totally defeated the acoustic torpedoes. Several-hundred GNATs were used by German submarines.

## 3. FIDO

Fido was the U.S. air-dropped anti-submarine torpedo that had acoustic guidance for homing on the propeller noises of submarines. First employed in Atlantic anti-submarine operations during World War II, the weapon was highly effective against submerged U-boats. It was used by land-based aircraft, especially the B-24 Liberator and PBY Catalina, and carrier based planes. The Fido's combat debut occurred in the Atlantic in May 1943 when a Liberator from the RAF

Coastal Command heavily damaged the *U-456*, which surfaced and was soon destroyed by convoy escort ships. The next day an RAF Liberator sank the submarine *U-266* with a Fido. During 1943–1945 some 340 Fido torpedoes were used against U-boats; they sank 68 submarines and damaged another 33, a very high success rate for an anti-submarine weapon. Allied aircraft using depth charges against U-boats achieved a 9.5 percent kill rate compared to 22 percent for Fido torpedoes. Fido was designated as the Mark 24 mine to disguise its true capabilities. The existence of Fido was unknown to the German Navy until after the war had ended. Fido's guidance was based on four passive hydrophones. When dropped into the water from an aircraft the Fido dived to a pre-set depth and began an acoustic search for the submarine, the torpedo's effective detection range being approximately 1,500 yards. If no propeller sounds were heard the torpedo would begin a circular search, which it could maintain for 10 to 15 minutes. At least one submarine, the *U-296*, was sunk by a Fido after a run of 13 minutes. On another occasion, against the *U-1107*, a Fido entered the water only 80 yards from the submarine but ran for three minutes before exploding, apparently having not made initial detection of the submarine but having gone into a circular search pattern before finding its target. Development of the Fido had begun in 1940 by a team headed by the Western Electric Co. Approximately 4,000 of these torpedoes were produced during the war. They remained in U.S. Navy service until 1948.

### 4. HUMAN TORPEDOES

In the latter half of 1942, with the Japanese Navy moving to the defensive, two naval officers—Ens. Sekio Nishina and Lt.(jg) Hiroski Kuroki—conceived of the *kaiten* or "human torpedo" based on the large Type 93 torpedo (see below). Permission was given for them to develop the weapon *only* if a means were provided for the pilot to escape at the last moment. In February 1944 the Naval General Staff gave permission to produce the kaiten and 100 torpedoes were converted in 1944 and 230 in 1945. Late in the war, several destroyers were modified to launch two or four kaitens over the stern and a light cruiser was provided with rails to launch eight kaitens. Also, several large submarines were modified to carry four kaitens, with the pilots able to move from the submarines into their torpedoes through a hatch connection while the mother submarine was submerged. Submarine-launched kaitens attacked several U.S. ships, but their only successes were sinking a tanker (with 50 of her crew killed) and a destroyer escort (with the death of 113 Americans). Several Japanese submarines and numerous kaitens were lost in scoring those two successes. The one-man kaitens weighed 18½ tons submerged, were 48 feet long, and had oxygen-kerosene engines that could drive them up to 30 knots, and for 85,000 yards at slower speeds. Their warhead contained 3,400 pounds of high explosives.

## 5. LONG LANCE

The Japanese Type 93 Long Lance was the largest torpedo and probably fastest used by any navy in World War II. Its explosive charge of 1,080 pounds compared to 879½ pounds in the U.S. Mark 17 torpedo, the largest American torpedo of the war (although none was used in combat). The Long Lance torpedoes were carried in several classes of Japanese cruisers and destroyers. The secret to the Long Lance's high performance was the use of oxygen as the propellant. The French Navy had first considered using oxygen as a torpedo propellant, but abandoned the concept because of the hazard of accidental explosion. The British similarly rejected the concept, but the Japanese persevered and the Type 93 was approved for production in 1933 (year 2,593 of the Japanese calendar). It was believed that oxygen torpedoes would outrange naval guns, creating a revolution in naval tactics. By December 1941 the Japanese had produced some 1,350 Long Lance torpedoes, about one-half the total that would be manufactured.

The Long Lance weighed 5,952 pounds, was 29½ feet long, and 24 inches in diameter. (The standard Allied and Axis torpedoes were 21 inches in diameter.) The range varied with setting—21,900 yards at 48 to 50 knots, 35,000 yards at 40 to 42 knots, and 43,700 yards at 36 to 38 knots. A larger Type 93 Model 3 was put in production in 1945, but was not used in combat; it weighed 6,173 pounds and carried a warhead of 1,720 pounds or twice the largest U.S. torpedo warhead. With their great speed and range, and large warhead, they were highly effective against Allied warships in the early surface battles of the Pacific War.

### 6. NUCLEAR TORPEDOES

The world's first nuclear-armed torpedo was the Soviet T-5, launched from submarines against surface ships. Nuclear warheads in anti-ship torpedoes would improve their "kill" radius, meaning that a direct hit on an enemy ship would not be required. A nuclear warhead could thus compensate for poor acoustic homing by the torpedo or for last-minute maneuvering by the target, and later for overcoming countermeasures or decoys that could confuse a torpedo's guidance. With the RDS-9 nuclear warhead, the T-5 was test launched from a submarine in 1957; the nuclear explosion had a yield of ten kilotons at a distance of just over six miles from the launching submarine. (That warhead size was more than half the size of the Hiroshima and Nagasaki atomic bombs.) The T-5 was the first nuclear weapon to enter service in Soviet submarines, becoming operational in 1958 as the Type 53-58. It was a 21-inch diameter weapon.

In 1960—two years after the year the first Soviet nuclear torpedo became operational—the nuclear Mark 45 ASTOR (anti-submarine torpedo) entered service in U.S. submarines. There was American interest in a nuclear torpedo as early as 1943, but not until the mid-1950s was a nuclear "fish" initiated. The U.S. Mark 45 ASTOR—the only nuclear torpedo produced in the West—was a 19-inch diameter weapon, fitted with a W34 warhead of 20 kilotons. It was launched from the standard 21-inch torpedo tubes and had a speed of 40 knots with a maximum range of 15,000 yards. The wire-guided ASTOR had no homing capability and no contact or influence exploder; it was guided and detonated by signals sent from the submarine through its trailing wire. In a form of gallows humor, U.S. submariners often cited the ASTOR as having a probability of kill (Pk) of *two*—the target submarine *and* the launching submarine!

### 7. PEARL HARBOR TORPEDOES

Air-launched torpedoes tend to descend deeply in the water before rising up to their programmed depth. In the 1920s the Japanese Navy had pioneered the development of tactics that would enable torpedoes to be dropped from greater heights and faster aircraft speeds than could Western torpedo aircraft. Also, in 1939—before there was any idea of an attack on Pearl Harbor—the Japanese Navy began studying the problem of attacking ships in shallow water. When the Japanese planned the Pearl Harbor attack of December 7, 1941, their torpedoes would normally have gotten stuck in the shallow waters—40 feet in the main channels and less in most other areas within the harbor. The answer: The torpedo was fitted with frangible wooden extensions to the fins at the rear of the torpedo's tail assembly. The wooden fins would break off upon the torpedo's entry into the water, keeping it from diving too deep and into the bottom of Pearl Harbor. The modified torpedoes were put into production at Nagasaki in mid-September 1941. All required for the Pearl Harbor attack were not ready when the carriers departed their home base for the attack force rendezvous in the remote Kurile Islands. Accordingly, the carrier *Kaga* was delayed until November 18 to take on board the last of the modified torpedoes, which were distributed to other ships when she reached Tankan Bay in the Kuriles. At the time there were less than 300 aerial torpedoes of all types available in the Japanese Navy. Of those, about one-half were allocated to the six large carriers that attacked Pearl Harbor—40 were used in the attack; the remaining aerial torpedoes were shipped to Formosa and Indochina for use by land-based naval bombers.

## 8. SHKVAL

During World War II there was some rocket-propelled torpedo development in Germany and Italy. After the war, interest was shown in this type of weapon in the Soviet Union and the United States, but only the Soviet Union developed rocket-propelled torpedoes. The aircraft-launched RAT-52 torpedo of 1952, for use against surface ships, had an underwater speed of almost 70 knots; the air-launched anti-submarine torpedoes APR-1 and APR-2 used solid-rocket propulsion to attain speeds just over 60 knots. In 1960 development of a submarine-launched rocket torpedo began. It involved a solid-propellant rocket motor coupled with moving the weapon through the water surrounded by a gaseous envelope or "bubble" that is created by the torpedo's shape and sustained by the rocket's exhaust. This technique is known as "artificial cavitation." The preliminary design of the Shkval (squall) was completed as early as 1963 and a submarine began test launches in May 1966. The tests were halted in 1972 because

of problems, but after seven launches from the submarine
*S-65* in June–December 1976 the torpedo—given the designation VA-111—was declared ready for operational use in November 1977—some 17 years after the project was initiated.
The 21-inch-diameter torpedo is 27 feet long and weighs 5,950
pounds. Its estimated range is more than 10,000 yards at
approximately 200 knots. Initially fitted with a nuclear warhead, later variants have terminal guidance and a conventional, high-explosive warhead of 460 pounds. There were
later reports that a 300-knot version was under development.
Even the 200-knot weapon was beyond the capabilities of
U.S. torpedo countermeasures.

## 9. THE WORLD'S LARGEST

The largest torpedo known to have been proposed was the
Soviet T-15 nuclear torpedo for use against U.S. and British
naval bases! In 1949–1950 the development of a submarine-
launched nuclear torpedo was begun in the Soviet Union.
The torpedo was to carry a thermonuclear (hydrogen) warhead a distance of some 16 nautical miles. It would have a
diameter of just over five feet and a length of approximately
27 feet. The 40-ton underwater weapon would be propelled
to its target by a battery-powered electric motor, providing a
speed of about 30 knots. Obviously, a new submarine would
have to be designed to carry the torpedo—one torpedo per
submarine. The submarine carrying a T-15 would surface
immediately prior to launching the torpedo to determine its
precise location by stellar navigation and using radar to identify coastal landmarks. The long submerged distances that
the submarine would have to transit to reach its targets demanded that it have nuclear propulsion. This was the beginning of Project 627, the Soviet Navy's first nuclear submarine
(NATO codename November). The project was initiated

without knowledge—or approval—of senior naval officers. In the fall of 1952 Soviet dictator Josef Stalin formally approved the project. Stalin died in early 1953, and in 1955—in response to the Navy's objections and recommendations—the requirement for Project 627 was revised for attacks against enemy shipping, to be armed with conventional (high-explosive) torpedoes. The forward section of the submarine was redesigned for eight 21-inch torpedo tubes; with 12 reloads provided (the submarine carried a total of 20 weapons). Later nuclear-warhead 21-inch torpedoes were added to the loadout of conventional torpedoes.

## 10. WIRE GUIDANCE

Early in the Cold War the U.S. Navy realized that a "hunter-killer" submarine could detect a high-speed or snorkeling submarine at greater distances than the homing sonar fitted in the torpedo. Accordingly, in 1950 the Bureau of Ordnance awarded a contract for development of a wire-guided torpedo that would be guided by the launching submarine until the torpedo's sonar could acquire the target. The German Navy had started development in the field during World War II. In 1956 some 120 Mark 27 Model 4 acoustic homing torpedoes of wartime design were refitted with wire guidance (redesignated Mark 39 Model 1) for fleet familiarization. Although these torpedoes were too slow to successfully attack a fast, maneuvering submarine, the subsequent U.S. Mark 37 and Mark 48 anti-submarine torpedoes were wire guided. The guidance cable is payed out from both the submarine and torpedo; it breaks when the torpedo's acoustic guidance is activated. The Mark 48 Model 3 introduced TELECOM (tele-communications) to provide two-way data transmissions between submarine and torpedo; thus the torpedo can transmit acoustic data back to the submarine for processing.

The Soviet Navy soon followed with its own wire-guided torpedoes (and also developed smaller anti-submarine torpedoes with wire guidance that could be launched from helicopters). Other navies have developed submarine-launched, wire-guided "fish."

# Missiles

## 1. EXOCET

The French-produced Exocet missile was probably used by more nations than any other anti-ship missile. The weapon, which became operational in 1979, could be launched from aircraft, submarines, and surface ships, with the Argentine Navy also launching two Exocets from a trailer in the Falklands conflict of 1982. The Exocet proved to be a potent weapon in the Falklands. Five air-launched Exocets released by Super Étendard aircraft scored four hits—two (whose warheads did not detonate) sank the destroyer *Sheffield* and two sank the container ship *Atlantic Conveyor*, the latter loaded with helicopters and military supplies. One of two Exocets launched from the trailer damaged the British destroyer *Glamorgan*. The early Exocet missiles had a range of some 25 nautical miles when fired from a ship and more than 30 nautical miles when launched from an aircraft. It was a sea-skimming missile with a 364-pound, high-explosive warhead.

## 2. FX 1400

German glide bombs of World War II were the first guided missiles to sink warships. A glide bomb is unpowered, using small wings to extend its range; the weapon was guided by an observer in the launching plane, making it a guided missile. On August 27, 1943, German aircraft carrying HS 293 glide bombs attacked British ships south of Cape Finesterre on the Spanish coast. The glide bombs sank the British sloop *Egret* and inflicted heavy damage on the destroyer *Athabaskan*. But more potent was the FX 1400 missile—also known as Fritz X—developed by Dr. Max Kramer. It was a 3,100-pound, armor-piercing bomb that could be controlled by radio signals from the launching aircraft; the missile had four fixed stabilizing fins and an enlarged tail assembly. FX 1400 prototypes were ready for testing by early 1942. The bomb took 42 seconds to fall from 20,000 feet, with a flare indicating the glide path to the observer who controlled the weapon. On September 9, 1943, a German bomber launched an FX 1400 against the Italian battleship *Roma*, en route to Malta as part of the Italian capitulation. The bomb struck the ship, igniting fires that reached the magazines. The dreadnought blew up and sank, killing 1,255 on board. The nearby battleship *Italia* was struck by another FX 1400, but survived. Subsequently, FX 1400s struck and severely damaged the U.S. cruiser *Savannah* (CL 42). The Germans continued air attacks with glide bombs against Allied ships, the last being against ships off Normandy on June 8, 1944. It was a deadly introduction to the guided missile era. Both U.S. and British scientists rapidly developed devices to jam the FX 1400 guidance signals.

### 3. POLARIS

The Polaris missile series provided the West with its most survivable strategic weapon from 1960 to 1981, and was the basis for the subsequent Poseidon and Trident submarine-launched missiles. On February 8, 1957, the Chief of Naval Operations, Adm. Arleigh Burke—against the judgment of most senior naval officers—issued a requirement for a 1,500-

nautical-mile missile launched from a submarine to be operational by 1965. This range would enable a submarine in the Norwegian Sea to target the Soviet capital of Moscow. Under the direction of Rear Adm. William ("Red") Raborn, the Navy and Lockheed developed and deployed the initial Polaris A-1 missiles in the nuclear-propelled submarine *George Washington* (SSBN 598) in November 1961. The 16 nuclear-tipped missiles in the *G.W.* had a range of 1,200 nautical miles. But the A-2 variant, with a 1,500-mile range, became operational in submarines in 1962, and the A-3 variant, with a 2,500-mile range and a three-vehicle warhead, entered the fleet in 1964. The Polaris was launched from submerged submarines; at the height of the program the Navy had 41 submarines (the last delivered in 1967) armed with 656 Polaris missiles. The last Polaris missile was taken off alert in October 1981. The Royal Navy also procured the Polaris (with British nuclear warheads) for four nuclear-propelled submarines. Polaris was also considered for use in surface ships—a squadron of NATO-operated missile ships based on merchant hulls, and several U.S. and Italian cruisers had space reserved for Polaris missiles. In the event, the Polaris was only deployed in submarines.

### 4. R-11FM

The Soviet R-11 (NATO designations SS-1b Scud-A) was the world's first ballistic missile to be launched by a submarine. Entering Army service in 1956, the basic R-11 was a 4½-ton missile with a storable-liquid propellant that could deliver a 2,200-pound conventional warhead to a maximum range of 80 nautical miles. The R-11 was soon fitted with a nuclear warhead of about ten kilotons, which initially reduced the missile's range by about one-half. In 1953–1954 S. P. Korolev proposed a naval variant of the missile that would be fueled

The ballistic missile submarine *Henry Clay* (SSBN 625) launches a Polaris A-2 missile. *U.S. Navy*

by kerosene and nitric acid in place of the R-11's alcohol and liquid oxygen, which was less stable for long-term storage. The world's first ballistic missile carrying submarine was the *B-67* (NATO codename Zulu). She was modified with two R-11FM missile tubes fitted in the after end of an enlarged sail structure and had related control equipment installed. On September 16, 1955, in the White Sea, the submarine *B-67* launched the first ballistic missile ever to be fired from a submarine. The missile streaked 135 nautical miles to impact in the remote Novaya Zemlya test range. Although the weapon was operational from about 1959, according to Capt. 2nd Rank V.L. Berezovskiy: "The preparation to launch a missile took a great deal of time. Surfacing, observation of position, the steadying of compasses—somewhere around an hour and twenty or thirty minutes. This is a monstrously long time. . . .

The submarine could be accurately detected even before surfacing [to launch]." The U.S., Soviet, French, and Chinese Navies developed more advanced, underwater-launch missiles, but the RF-11FM was the first submarine-launched ballistic missile.

## 5. **REGULUS**

The Regulus guided (cruise) missile was the world's first submarine-launched weapon developed to attack land targets with a nuclear warhead. Building on German V-1 missile technology, the U.S. Navy developed the Regulus I, a turbojet-propelled, surface-launched weapon with a range of some 500 miles. It could also be used against surface ships, although that was a secondary role. The original payload was to be a 4,000-pound conventional warhead, but in the end the weapon went to sea with a nuclear warhead. Chance Vought delivered the first operational missiles in May 1954 for use from surface ships, and the following year the carrier *Hancock* (CVA 19) and heavy cruiser *Los Angeles* (CA 135) deployed to the Western Pacific with nuclear-armed Regulus missiles. The first submarine launch of a Regulus missile occurred on July 15, 1953, from the surfaced diesel-electric *Tunny* (SSG 282); but she did not go to sea on the first submarine missile patrol (with two missiles) until 1958. Cruisers and carriers embarked Regulus missiles only for a few years; four diesel-electric submarines and the nuclear *Halibut* (SSGN 587) carried Regulus missiles on patrol until 1964, when the Navy had sufficient Polaris missile submarines at sea. Regulus I was to be an interim weapon; the Regulus II was a supersonic, 1,000-mile missile that was to succeed the earlier weapon, with the Navy planning to build a dozen nuclear submarines for the weapon. Plans were also being drawn up for cruisers to carry the "Reg II." However, the development of the Polaris missile and the need to pay for that program led to cancellation of the Regulus II in December 1958. The U.S. Air Force briefly considered employing the Regulus II as an air-launched missile from B-52 bombers, and the French Navy considered using them from aircraft carriers.

## 6. SHADDOCK

The Soviet-developed P-5 missile (NATO codename SS-N-3 Shaddock) was a large, anti-ship missile fitted in numerous submarines and several cruisers. The weapon was originally developed—like the U.S. Regulus missile—for the strategic land-attack role. The Shaddock was fitted in a deck-mounted canister that performed both the storage and launch functions, simplifying installation in surface ships as well as submarines. This was in contrast to the U.S. Navy's method for the Regulus, which employed the canister as only a hangar, with the missile having to be manually extracted, placed on launch rails, wings extended, and other manual functions performed before launching. The first P-5 missile was launched from the converted *S-146* (NATO Whiskey class) on November 22, 1957, in the White Sea. After extensive tests the P-5 system became operational in 1959 and was installed in diesel-electric and nuclear-propelled submarines. The Shaddock could carry a 2,200-pound conventional or a nuclear warhead. The strategic land-attack role was soon dropped as ballistic missile submarines became available. Subsequently, the improved P-6 Shaddock was fitted in the submarines and surface ships. This was an anti-ship weapon with a range of 300 nautical miles. A reconnaissance aircraft could locate and target the ships, providing radar "pictures" to the missile ship via video data link. Later the Soviets also used satellites to target allied warships, especially aircraft carriers, for the Shaddock "shooters." The Shaddock was considered a particular threat to U.S. and British aircraft carriers. More advanced versions of the surface-launched Shaddock were deployed, later replaced by submerged-launch missiles. The Soviets converted or built 22 diesel-electric submarines, 35 nuclear submarines, and several surface ships to carry the Shaddock.

## 7. SIDEWINDER

The U.S. Navy-developed Sidewinder missile was the West's principal air-to-air weapon during the Cold War. The Sidewinder was the most widely used missile in the West with several hundred thousand Sidewinders having been produced for some 40 nations in addition to the United States. Developed by the naval weapons center at China Lake, California, the Sidewinder is a simple, effective, infrared-homing missile. The Sidewinder became operational in 1956. It was used to score most of the air-to-air kills by U.S. Navy and Air Force aircraft in the Vietnam War, and by the Israeli Air Force in the 1967 and 1973 wars in the Middle East. During the 1982 fighting over Lebanon's Bekaa Valley, Israeli aircraft used Sidewinders to shoot down 51 of 55 Syrian-flown MiG aircraft destroyed in aerial combat. The Sidewinder was also highly successfully when used by British Harrier VSTOL aircraft in the 1982 Falklands conflict. The solid-propellant missile has a range of about ten nautical miles and carries a 21- to 25-pound warhead. It is compatible with virtually all Western fighters and some attack aircraft as well as helicopters. Periodically there have been proposals to provide a submarine-launched version of the missile, dubbed "Subwinder." But to date no action has been taken on this proposal.

## 8. STYX

The P-15 missile (NATO designation SS-N-2 Styx) was developed for the Soviet Navy to provide an anti ship missile capability for small combat craft in the coastal defense role. The Styx—which became operational in 1958—gained international attention after Egyptian Komar missile boats, from just outside of Port Said harbor, sank the Israeli destroyer *Eilat* steaming 13½ nautical miles offshore on October 21, 1967. The weapon was subsequently used by the Indian Navy to sink a number of Pakistani ships in the 1971 Indo-Pakistani conflict, including the destroyer *Khaiber*. The Styx was a subsonic missile propelled by a turbojet engine with a solid-fuel booster; range was 25-plus nautical miles carrying a conventional, 1,100-pound warhead. The guidance in the early versions was terminal radar homing. The proliferation of Styx missiles to several communist and neutral states led the U.S. Navy to initiate several missile defense systems including the Sea Sparrow missile and Phalanx close-in weapon system (CIWS).

## 9. TERRIER

The Terrier was the West's first surface-to-air missile. Development began late in World War II under Project Bumblebee, which evolved into three missiles—the short range Tartar, medium-range Terrier, and long-range Talos. The latter two missiles could be fitted with nuclear warheads. The Terrier became operational in 1955 aboard the converted U.S. cruisers *Boston* (CAG 1) and *Canberra* (CAG 2). A nuclear warhead for the BTN (beam-riding Terrier nuclear) became available in 1962. Approximately 8,000 Terrier missiles of all models were produced by 1966 when production ended. They were fitted in three U.S. aircraft carriers and a large number of cruisers and destroyers, plus several Dutch and Italian warships. The Terrier, with a range of 20 to 40 nautical miles, was a two-stage, solid-propellant missile. It served as the principal U.S. shipboard air defense missile into the 1980s, when it was replaced by the Standard-series missiles. Some Terrier variants were also suitable for the anti-ship role.

## 10. **TOMAHAWK**

The Tomahawk is a U.S. long-range cruise missile developed for both surface and submarine launch against both surface ship and land targets. It was initially known as the sea-launched cruise missile (SLCM) and intended for nuclear strike against the Soviet Union. In 1979 the Navy began using the terms Tomahawk land-attack missile (TLAM) and Tomahawk anti-ship missile (TASM) to distinguish the principal variants. (It was also evaluated for air launch, but the Air Force rejected the missile for its bombers.) The subsonic missile became operational in 1982. Its flexibility is demonstrated by the large number of surface ships and submarines that can fire the weapon, the latter from vertical launch tubes or from standard, 21-inch torpedo tubes. Also, the Tomahawk could be fitted with 1,000-pound conventional warheads, or warheads with 166 small bomblets or carbon-fiber spools for knocking out power stations, or a W80 nuclear warhead. The Intermediate-range Nuclear Force Treaty of 1987 led to all nuclear TLAMs being taken ashore; the conventional anti-ship missiles have also been beached. Since 1991 conventional land-attack missiles have been launched by U.S. submarines and surface ships, and by British submarines against targets in Iraq, Afghanistan, and Sudan. The TLAM variants have a range of almost 1,000 miles, with the latest variants capable of being retargeted while in flight.

# nuclear Weapons

The U.S. Navy was involved in the development of nuclear weapons from almost the start of the Manhattan Project in 1942. Capt. William ("Deak") Parsons, a Navy ordnance expert, was given responsibility for transforming the plutonium and uranium nuclear "devices" developed at Los Alamos into combat weapons. Subsequently, Parsons, as the bomb commander, flew on the B-29 *Enola* Gay carrying the Little Boy atomic bomb dropped on Hiroshima on August 6, 1945. His colleague, Comdr. John T. ("Chic") Hayward, flew in the same role on the B-29 *Bockscar* that dropped the Fat Man atomic bomb on Nagasaki on August 9, 1945. After the war the Navy sought to obtain nuclear weapons because many national defense policy makers believed that future wars would be fought with atomic weapons. Within the Navy some senior officers believed that the Navy had to acquire nuclear weapons to have a role in future defense policy decisions and in future conflicts.

## 1. FIRST NUCLEAR WEAPON

The first nuclear weapon provided for naval use—the Atomic Energy Commission retained control of the nuclear components—was the Mk 7, which became available in 1952. It was carried by P2V-3C Neptune bombers, which could take off from but not land aboard aircraft carriers, and then the AJ Savage attack aircraft, which was fully carrier capable.

## 2. FIRST SURFACE-TO-SURFACE MISSILE

The world's first nuclear surface-to-surface cruise or guided missile was the U.S. Navy's Regulus, which became operational in 1954, aboard cruisers. Subsequently, the Regulus was deployed on aircraft carriers and on five submarines— four diesel-electric and one, the USS *Halibut* (SSGN 587), nuclear propelled. The Regulus had a subsonic speed and range of 500 miles and carried a nuclear warhead, initially the Mk 5 but later the W27.

## 3. LARGEST NUCLEAR BOMBER

The largest nuclear-capable aircraft to regularly operate from aircraft carriers was the U.S. Navy's A3D Skywarrior (redesignated A-3 in 1962). The aircraft had a takeoff weight of 73,000 pounds in the bomber configuration, able to carry a nuclear bomb internally, or up to 12,000 pounds of conventional bombs. The Douglas A3D served in the U.S. Navy from March 1956 to 1991. The tanker variants (KA-3) weighed slightly more.

## 4. SMALLEST NUCLEAR BOMBER

The smallest carrier-based aircraft to carry a nuclear weapon was the Douglas A4D Skyhawk (later redesignated A-4). Operational in the attack role from September 1956 to June 1992, it was the smallest carrier-based attack aircraft of the nuclear era with an empty weight of 9,146 pounds and maximum carrier takeoff weight of 22,500 pounds in the A4D-2N (A-4C) variant. It could carry a single nuclear bomb or 9,000 pounds of conventional bombs, missiles, and rockets.

## 5. FIRST nUCLEAR GUN

Only two nuclear projectiles are known to have been developed for naval guns. The Soviet Navy produced nuclear rounds for the 6-inch (152-mm) guns of the 14 *Sverdlov*-class cruisers completed in 1951–1955 (12 guns per ship). The date that the nuclear rounds became available for those guns is not known. The U.S. Navy developed a nuclear projectile with the Mk 23 warhead for the 16-inch (406-mm) guns of the four U.S. *Iowa* (BB 61) class battleships. The ships each had nine guns. The 16-inch nuclear rounds were in the inventory from December 1956 to October 1962.

## 6. FIRST nUCLEAR TORPEDO

The world's first nuclear-armed torpedo was the Soviet T-5, which entered service in 1958 as the Type 53-58. The weapon had a range in excess of six miles carrying an RDS-9 nuclear warhead. The West's only nuclear torpedo was the U.S. Navy's Mk 45 ASTOR—anti-submarine torpedo—which became operational in 1960; it carried the W34 warhead.

## 7. FIRST SURFACE-TO-AIR MISSILE

The first nuclear surface-to-air missile aboard ship was the U.S. Talos, which was fitted to seven guided missile cruisers, one, the USS *Long Beach* (CGN 9), being nuclear propelled. The Talos became operational with the W30 nuclear warhead in February 1959.

## 8. FIRST BALLISTIC MISSILE

The world's first sea-launch ballistic missile with a nuclear warhead was the Soviet R-11 (NATO designations SS-1b Scud-A). The R-11FM entered service and went to sea in submarines around 1959 carrying a nuclear warhead of about ten kilotons. Its range was on the order of 80 miles. It was soon replaced in Soviet submarines by nuclear missiles with better performance and, eventually, submerged launch. The first U.S. Navy ballistic missile was the Polaris A-1, which went to sea in submarines in 1960 with a range of 1,380 miles. The missile carried a W47 nuclear warhead. Improved missiles of the Polaris series, followed by the Poseidon and Trident missiles, went to sea in U.S. submarines.

### 9. FIRST NUCLEAR MINE

The Soviet Union is the only nation to have developed a nuclear sea mine. Few details of the device are available, but the original plan to bring Soviet forces and weapons into Cuba—which precipitated the Cuban missile crisis of 1962—included two nuclear mines to protect Cuban coastal waters from U.S. ship and submarine intrusions. The British considered developing such a weapon, but it was not pursued.

### 10. LARGEST SHIPBOARD MISSILE

The largest sea-launched nuclear missile is the Soviet RSM-52 (NATO designation SS-N-20 Sturgeon), developed to be launched from the giant Soviet Typhoon nuclear-propelled submarines. The RSM-52, which became operational in 1983, weighs 177,000 pounds and is 52 ½ feet long. The missile has a range of 5,150 miles and can carry up to ten reentry vehicles of about 100 kilotons each. The largest U.S. sea-launched missile is the Trident D-5, which is carried in the *Ohio* (SSBN 726) class submarines. Operational since 1990, the missile weighs 130,000 pounds and is 44 feet long. It has a range of almost 4,600 miles and can carry up to eight W88 reentry vehicles of an estimated 450 kilotons each.

# Attacks on Ships in Peacetime

## 1. THE AMERICAN FRIGATE *CHESAPEAKE*

The British and French remained locked in warfare in the early 19th Century, with the British in particular gaining wide notoriety for the practice of impressment—kidnapping unwilling men to serve in the crews of the Royal Navy's warships. When possible, such impressed sailors often deserted. British warships frequently stopped ships of all nations to look for deserters. In June 1807 off the coast of Virginia, the British frigate *Leopard* ordered the American frigate *Chesapeake* to stop and be searched and, when the Americans refused to do so, opened fire. Three Americans men were killed and 18, including the captain, were wounded, and the ship was badly damaged. The British carried out their search, carting off four men, only one of whom was an actual deserter. U.S. diplomats protested but the British ignored the complaints. Rancor in the United States over the affair never abated, however, and was a major factor in the decision five years later to go to war with Britain. The *Chesapeake* had one more role to play in the subsequent War of 1812, and in 1813 was captured in battle with another British frigate, despite its dying captain's exhortation, "Don't Give Up The Ship!"

## 2. THE *TRENT* AFFAIR

Intent on striking a blow at the Confederacy and on stirring up a potential conflict with the British, Capt. Charles Wilkes, commander of the U.S. warship *San Jacinto*, intercepted the British merchant ship *Trent* off of Cuba in October 1861. It was known that two Confederate diplomatic agents, John Slidell and James Mason, were aboard the British ship, bound for London to enlist Britain and France in the southerners' cause. The *San Jacinto* fired on the *Trent* to compel her to stop and, despite vigorous protests by the British, American sailors and Marines boarded the British ship and carried off the southerners. Although public opinion and Congress heartily approved of Wilkes' actions, President Abraham Lincoln and his administration immediately realized that the move was illegal, and quickly presented apologies to the British while offering to return the prisoners. The Union government declared Wilkes to have acted without instructions and the British, while displaying great umbrage in its communications, ultimately accepted the apologies and Slidell and Mason were allowed to continue on their mission.

## 3. "REMEMBER THE *MAINE!*"

When the American battleship *Maine* blew up on the night of February 15, 1898, while anchored in the harbor of Havana, Cuba, U.S. media speculation immediately turned to a purported plot by Spanish authorities. Tensions over the island between the United States and Spain had been heating up; to the U.S.-supported independence-minded Cuban separatists, the battleship's presence was a political statement of U.S. interest. While no evidence was found to implicate the Spaniards in the explosion, which killed 260 American sailors and marines, U.S. public opinion was convinced of Spain's guilt, and two months later war was declared. Spain was soundly defeated in the ensuing conflict, which liberated Cuba, garnered Puerto Rico, Guam, and the Philippines for the United States, largely ended Spain's presence in the New World, and established the United States as a major international power. In 1976, Adm. Hyman G. Rickover published a detailed scientific study on the explosion and concluded that it was not a result of Spanish activity, but was due to spontaneous combustion of coal near an ammunition magazine. Other authorities have questioned his findings.

## 4. SINKING OF THE *LUSITANIA*

The 32,000-ton British ocean liner *Lusitania* was one of the grandest ships in the world, famous ever since she came on the North Atlantic scene in 1907. But the ship's sinking on May 1, 1915, by the German submarine *U-20* killed 1,195 passengers and crew, including 123 citizens of the then-neutral United States. The world's horror at the man-made tragedy forever linked the ship's name to infamy. Germans felt that the sinking was justified, as they had intelligence that the merchant ship was illegally carrying arms from the United States to Britain and therefore was a legitimate target. Whether or not the ship was carrying contraband munitions remains controversial to this day, but in any case public opinion in the United States—home of millions of German immigrants—turned distinctly anti-German following the sinking. Congress was incensed, but it would be another two years (and a presidential election) before President Woodrow Wilson asked for a declaration of war and the United States entered World War I against Germany.

## 5. ATTACK ON THE U.S. GUNBOAT *PANAY*

In late 1937 Japanese forces were relentlessly advancing on the Chinese government's wartime capital at Nanking, far up the Yangtze River, and the last group of diplomats from the American embassy embarked in the U.S. river gunboat *Panay* (PR 5) to evacuate the capital. The *Panay* was one of six shallow-draft river gunboats built in China for the U.S. Navy in the late 1920s. In 1937, as the Japanese and Nationalist Chinese fought, several large American flags had been painted on the gunboats to identify them as a neutral, but on December 12 Japanese aircraft attacked and dropped 18 bombs on and around the *Panay*. The crew and passengers were strafed with machine gun fire as they abandoned ship and reached shore, and three American sailors and an Italian passenger were killed, and 43 other Navymen and 5 civilians were wounded. The Japanese government promptly apologized for the incident, fired an officer and offered to pay restitution to the victims. Despite clear evidence that the attack was deliberate, the United States accepted the apologies and payments, and war with Japan was temporarily averted.

### 6. SINKING OF THE GREEK CRUISER *HELLE*

Italian dictator Benito Mussolini was agitating in the summer of 1940 for an excuse to attack Greece. Italian government-controlled newspapers and radio charged that British forces at war with Italy were routinely using Greek islands for bases—a violation of neutrality. On August 15, 1940, the Italian submarine *Delfino* launched torpedoes at the small Greek cruiser *Helle,* anchored at the Aegean island of Tinos. Nine men died as the ship sank in the harbor, and the Italian media blamed the British. Popular opinion in Greece, however, blamed Italy for the sinking and ironically increased sentiment for supporting the British. Greece was too weak to respond militarily, and did little more than protest. Two months later Italy declared war on its Balkan neighbor. Germany would have to enter the fray to help its ally Italy, an action that would delay the German invasion of Soviet Russia in the summer of 1941. That delay would force the Germans to fight in the severe winter of 1941–1942, contributing to the failure of their Russian campaign.

## 7. THE SIEGE OF THE *AMETHYST*

The British public was transfixed in the spring and summer of 1949 by the siege of the *Amethyst*, a Royal Navy sloop (escort ship) trapped up the Yangtze River by Chinese communist forces. The warship, en route to Nanking, was damaged by communist gunfire on April 20 and spent several days aground and under fire. Twenty-two men were killed—including the captain—and more than 30 men were wounded. After being refloated the ship moved upriver and anchored. For the next ten weeks the Chinese refused to allow any supplies to reach the ship while demanding the British admit that they were wrongly in China and had started the gun fight. Britain refused to do so, and during the night of July 30 the *Amethyst* began a 104-mile downriver dash to freedom. While the exploits of the crew were widely cheered in the West, the incident heralded the end of the presence of British, American, and French warships on China's rivers and marked an early flashpoint in what would be known as the Cold War.

## 8. TONKIN GULF INCIDENT EXPLODES INTO WAR

Elements in the American government in mid-1964 were searching for ways to intensify U.S. participation in the conflict in Vietnam and directly attack communist North Vietnam, and U.S. Navy destroyers began a series of provocative patrols close to North Vietnam's territorial waters in the Gulf of Tonkin. On August 2 one of those destroyers, the *Maddox* (DD 731), was attacked by three North Vietnamese torpedo boats, and supporting U.S. carrier aircraft attacked the craft. Two days later, the *Maddox*, joined by the destroyer *Turner*

*Joy* (DD 951), picked up numerous surface contacts on radar, and the two ships spent several hours in high-speed maneuvers and shooting in the dark. Despite the lack of confirmed enemy sightings in this second incident, President Lyndon Johnson ordered retaliatory air attacks on North Vietnam and declared that communist forces had deliberately attacked the U.S. ships in international waters. The resulting Tonkin Gulf resolution passed by Congress on August 7 authorized the use of military force in Southeast Asia without a declaration of war. The *Maddox* had been on a provocative spy mission at the time of the first attack and she was in fact attacked by North Vietnamese torpedo boats although in international waters. There was, however, no attack by the North Vietnamese on August 4.

## q. ATTACKED BY A FRIEND—THE SPY SHIP *LIBERTY*

The United States was intensely interested in Soviet activity in the Middle East as Israel attacked its hostile neighbors during the Six-Day War of 1967. The Pentagon ordered the electronic intelligence ship *Liberty* (AGTR 5) close to the coast of Sinai to get a better idea of what was going on with Soviet forces in Egypt (the *Liberty* had Russian and Arabic linguists on board, but no Hebrew speakers). On June 8, Israeli aircraft and torpedo boats attacked the American ship in international waters off the Sinai coast, killing 34 U.S. Navy sailors and wounding 171 during a sustained attack. Israel claimed it was all a case of mistaken identity and that the *Liberty* was thought to be an Egyptian ship. The U.S. government accepted that conclusion after several U.S. and Israeli investigations. The incident continues to stir controversy and deep emotions in the United States and in Israel. A multitude of conspiracy theories have produced a number of plausible and unlikely scenarios, and a number of survivors among the crew continue to press for renewed investigations. The *Liberty*'s commanding officer, Comdr. William L. McGonagle, was awarded the Medal of Honor for his and his crew's heroism on that tragic day.

## 10. NORTH KOREA CAPTURES THE *PUEBLO*

Only a few months after the *Liberty* incident another American spy ship found itself surrounded and under fire by hostile forces, and, although just one sailor was killed, the outcome was worse: for the first time since the surrender of the *Chesapeake* in 1807, an American naval ship hauled down its flag to an enemy on the high seas. The USS *Pueblo* (AGER 2) was a smaller ship than the *Liberty*, but also crammed with electronic interception gear to monitor enemy communications. Cruising about 15 miles off the North Korean coast on what the U.S. Navy thought was a routine Cold War espionage mission, the ship was surrounded by four communist naval ships, which opened fire and boarded the American vessel. With virtually no armament and no support from other forces, the commanding officer, Comdr. Lloyd Bucher, chose to surrender to try to save the lives of his crew. The ship's capture was a major intelligence coup for the North Koreans, and a great deal of secret equipment and records was captured despite attempts by the crew to destroy the material. The crew was made prisoners and paraded before the international press as war criminals. The United States, increasingly mired in the Vietnam War and, a week after the capture, heavily involved in beating back the Communist Tet offensive, was in no mood for armed confrontation with the North Koreans, and after nearly a year managed to negotiate a return of the 83 American prisoners. The *Pueblo* herself was turned into a museum ship by the communists, and the U.S. Navy ended its spy ship program.

# Battles That Changed History

Some of these battles changed the fate of nations, others affected entire civilizations. History would have turned out quite differently were it not for the outcomes of these naval actions.

## 1. SALAMIS (480 BC)

Athenians destroyed 200 Persian ships in a few hours, turning back the immediate threat of invasion and leading to the withdrawal of all Persian land forces from Greece. The Athenian victory caused the Persians to forever end their efforts to conquer the Greek city-states and preserved Greek independence.

## 2. LEPANTO (OCTOBER 7, 1571)

Christian Mediterranean nations put aside their differences and united to defeat the Islamic Turks in an epic struggle to decide who would rule the eastern Mediterranean. Nearly 500 ships from both sides fought near the Gulf of Patras, but the outnumbered Christians carried the day. About 20,000 Turks died along with 8,000 Christians, and the Muslim threat waned after this last "crusade" by the European Christians. The battle also marked the last widespread use of oared galleys, a staple of Mediterranean warfare since the days of the Phoenicians.

## 3. **THE SPANISH ARMADA (1588)**

In a David-vs.-Goliath struggle, the fledgling English fleet in the summer of 1588 went up against the naval might of Spain, the premier maritime power of the day. More than 130 Spanish ships carrying about 26,000 men advanced through the English Channel with orders to convoy another 30,000 troops from the Spanish Netherlands to invade Britain. But days of pinprick gunfights, a nightmarish attack by fire ships, and a fleet action off Gravelines, France, in which the English demonstrated superior gunnery, all combined to whittle down the Spanish fleet and make invasion impossible. The Spaniards continued home by circling around the British Isles, where many of their ships were driven ashore by storms. By the time the Armada reached home about half its ships had been sunk and more than 10,000 men killed. Pride from the English victory lasted for years and heartened those throughout Europe fighting Spain, which never again seriously threatened Britain.

## 4. **BATTLE OF THE CHESAPEAKE (SEPTEMBER 5, 1781)**

One might think that the only major defeat of the British Navy in two hundred years, a victory by a traditional also-ran that cemented the independence of the nascent United States, would be better remembered, but it is not so. Among the probable causes are that the battle between ships was brief and inconclusive, but the inability of the British to force their way past a French fleet into Chesapeake Bay, support the army of Gen. Charles Cornwallis, and attack the American forces under George Washington led to Britain's defeat in the American War of Independence. French Adm. Comte de Grasse and his fleet did not have long to enjoy their victory; a British fleet defeated the French the following April and de Grasse was taken prisoner.

## 5. TRAFALGAR (OCTOBER 21, 1805)

This remains the most famous battle in British naval history, cementing forever in British hearts both Adm. Lord Horatio Nelson and the Royal Navy. Nelson, at the cost of his life, capped a storied career by soundly defeating a combined French and Spanish fleet off the Spanish coast. The British fleet of 27 ships-of-the-line smashed the 33-ship combined fleet, sinking or capturing 22 of the enemy. Without that fleet Napoleon could not guarantee the safety of his army in a crossing of the English Channel, and the threat of invasion of England was averted. By dying in victory, Nelson's reputation took on almost mythic proportions.

## 6. THE *MONITOR* VS. THE *MERRIMAC* (MARCH 9, 1862)

This indecisive action between two ships was fought between warships unlike anything the world had ever seen before, and dramatically altered the shape of naval warfare for most of the next century. Confederates at Norfolk, Virginia, completely rebuilt a sunken Union frigate, the *Merrimac*, into an armored ram they renamed the *Virginia*. Up north, the Union contracted with eccentric Swedish immigrant inventor John Ericsson to hastily build a unique, turreted armored ship called the *Monitor*. During an epic one-on-one struggle in Hampton Roads, Virginia, neither ship could strike a decisive blow, but the Confederates were prevented from doing more damage to the otherwise defenseless Union fleet. The *Virginia* was scuttled by the Confederates rather than risk her capture. The battle caught world attention, confirmed Ericsson's belief that the turret was the most superior way to mount guns in a warship, and led to the block obsolescence of every wooden sailing warship.

## 7. JUTLAND (MAY 31–JUNE 1, 1916)

By far the largest naval engagement of World War I, the action of Denmark's Jutland brought together the two mightiest fleets of the day, the British Grand Fleet and the German High Seas Fleet. But after two days of intense but brief encounters, the British chased the Germans back into port and, despite the total loss of five capital ships and more than 8,500 sailors, little of consequence changed. Both sides claimed victory—the Germans had a numerical advantage in sinking three British battle cruisers to their one, plus an older battleship, and more than twice as many British sailors were killed as German. But the German fleet never again challenged the British on the high seas and ceased to be a real factor in the war. The battle's most lasting effect might have been the volumes written about it and the excessive study it engendered among the world's naval professionals, who spent much of the ensuing two decades thinking about rectifying the commanders' many mistakes.

## 8. MIDWAY (JUNE 4–5, 1942)

One of the great victories of all time hinged on luck—a group of American dive bombers found an enemy carrier force that was virtually undefended at that moment. With the inordinately opportune moment, the American SBD Dauntless dive bombers led by Lt. Comdr. Clarence McClusky took immediate advantage of the situation. The four Japanese fleet carriers, which had destroyed virtually all before them the previous six months, were sunk with all of their aircraft. The Americans had been losing the war and the battle until their Dauntless dive bombers screamed down on the Japanese and the tide of the conflict changed in a few short minutes, rightly earning the oft-used description, "miracle at Midway." Although Japan could replace its four lost aircraft carriers and their aircraft, it was never able to recreate the expertise lost with their pilots and aircrews.

## 9. BATTLE OF THE ATLANTIC (SEPTEMBER 1939–MAY 1945)

Not until March 1941 did British Prime Minister Winston Churchill came up with a name for the vicious campaign that pitted Allied convoys at sea against German submarines, but the conflict was the longest campaign of World War II and one of the most decisive conflicts of all time. The allies—principally Britain and the Soviet Union—would not be able to continue fighting Nazi Germany without the crucial supplies coming primarily from the United States, and the battle was a desperate one on all sides. Numerous technical and tactical developments saw both sides gaining superiority, but not until mid-1943, when air power was extended into the mid-Atlantic, did the Allies gain a lasting advantage. The losses were staggering: more than 30,000 Allied merchant sailors died and about 3,000 cargo ships were sunk—around 14.5 million gross tons—along with about 175 warships. German losses were even more severe: 783 submarines were lost along with about 28,000 sailors, or about four out of every five U-boat sailors—the highest casualty rate of any armed service during the war.

## 10. LEYTE GULF (OCTOBER 20–26, 1945)

The actions for Leyte Gulf comprised the largest naval battle of all time; the last fleet action fought by the Imperial Japanese Navy; the last battleship-vs-battleship action; the debut of the kamikaze suicide aircraft; and the only time Japanese surface ships sank an American aircraft carrier. This epic struggle took place as the Americans returned to the Philippines after being defeated in early 1942 by the Japanese. This time around, the invasion of Leyte was accompanied by the virtual destruction of what remained of Japan's sea power

An Allied aircraft attacks a surfaced U-boat in the Battle of the Atlantic. *U.S. Navy*

as Japan sacrificed the remainder of its aircraft carriers—largely without aircraft—as decoys to allow its battleships to get in close to the invasion fleet. One group of Japanese battlewagons actually did so and briefly terrorized a group of small escort carriers, but a determined counterattack by American escorts drove off the Japanese. Virtually every major Japanese ship that survived was seriously damaged and the Japanese Navy ceased to be a major factor in the war.

# Amphibious Landings

The Phoenicians in the Mediterranean and the Vikings in northern Europe were among many ancient peoples who spread their power and influence via assault from the sea. But until well into the 20th Century, seaborne assault was a risky, haphazard, extemporized affair, often using ships and tactics thrown together for the task at hand. Nevertheless, the results could be dramatic, changing the course of campaigns, wars, and history. Many invasions from the sea took place initially without a fight. These are some of the more significant amphibious assaults of defended shores.

## 1. FORT FISHER (1865)

The assault by Union forces on the Confederate Fort Fisher in January 1865 was in many ways the progenitor of the modern joint amphibious assault. The fort, an impressive network of earthworks, guarded Wilmington, North Carolina, the last open port of the Confederacy. A bombardment by Union warships, begun early on January 13, was followed by troop landings. More than 5,000 Union troops, sailors, and Marines battled over the next two days, continually assisted by naval gunfire, until the fort surrendered late on the 15th. Smooth

Army-Navy cooperation contributed heavily to the Union victory, a condition attributed to the commanders, Rear Adm. David Dixon Porter and Maj. Gen. Alfred H. Terry, even though the two had quarreled before the campaign.

## 2. GALLIPOLI (1915)

One of the all-time great, "how *not* to invade an enemy's shores" campaigns, Gallipoli has become synonymous with unmitigated disaster. An assault on the Dardenelles—the passage between European and Asian Turkey between the Mediterranean and Black Seas—was dreamed up by First Lord of the Admiralty Winston Churchill, who saw it as a way to provide some much-needed support to the Russians on the Eastern Front and break the stalemate that had become the Western Front. The Allies figured Turkey for an easy target, and figured quite wrong. A February 19, 1915, assault on the Turkish forts by a fleet of old British and French battleships failed miserably as three battleships were sunk and three others heavily damaged. A land assault was then planned, but after Allied troops came ashore on April 25, the Turks—numbering over 84,000 troops—fought tough as nails and slaughtered many of the British, Australian, New Zealand, and French troops that came ashore on several beaches at Cape Helles. At great cost the Allies gained the narrowest of footholds along the cliffs and beaches at the shoreline, but months of combat failed to move the front inland. Realizing the campaign was a failure, the Allies embarked upon the only successful portion of the entire effort and evacuated the bulk of 14 divisions in December—without the Turks becoming aware that the Allies were leaving. Eight months of some of the most vicious fighting of World War I saw 100,000 soldiers killed from all sides with more than 237,000 wounded. Down Under, the bravery displayed by Australian and New Zealand Army Corps (ANZAC) soldiers is considered by many to mark the true emergence of a national identity in those countries, and April 25, ANZAC Day, is a national holiday in both nations. The Gallipoli disaster forced Churchill's resignation from the government.

### 3. JAPANESE ASSAULTS OF WORLD WAR II (1941–1942)

The island nation of Japan was long accustomed to planning and carrying out amphibious assaults, and the techniques and equipment developed by the Japanese prior to World War II were likely the most sophisticated in the world. All this came into play on December 8, 1942 (the other side of the dateline during the December 7 attack on Pearl Harbor) when Japanese amphibious forces were unleashed on an unprecedented scale across the western Pacific. In rapid-fire succession, near-simultaneous amphibious landings were made on Guam and Wake Island in the Central Pacific, in the northern Philippine Islands, on the Malay Peninsula, the Aleutian Islands, and elsewhere. It was an impressive display of military might by a country greatly underestimated by many of the Western powers. All the assaults ultimately were successful, and in a few weeks the Japanese empire completely dominated a vast swath of the western Pacific region.

### 4. OPERATION SEA LION (1940)

The expected success of the threatened German invasion of England in the fall of 1940 was one of the most serious threats to the cause of the Allied democratic powers, but in the end it became one of the great invasions that never were. The Germans, having swept through Western Europe in the blitzkrieg campaign of the spring and summer of 1940, literally gazed across the English Channel at their next conquest, and a great assemblage of craft from all over the continent began as the

Nazis prepared for their first major seaborne assault. But control of the air was needed before they could attempt the channel crossing, and the previously dominant Luftwaffe found itself stymied by the hard-pressed Royal Air Force. "Never in the course of human events," said British Prime Minister Winston Churchill, "have so many owed so much to so few," and the German Air Force was beaten back with staggering losses to its bomber crews. With no prospect of securing air superiority, the Germans essentially declared a loss of interest in invading England, and, like Napoleon in the early 1800s, soon turned their attention east, toward Russia.

## 5. U.S. PACIFIC CAMPAIGNS (1942–1945)

For more than 30 years before the outbreak of war with Japan in 1941, the United States envisioned a campaign that would fight its way across thousands of miles of the western Pacific toward a decisive battle near the Japanese home islands. Detailed first by a remarkable visionary, Marine Corps Lt. Col. Earl ("Pete") Ellis, the plan by 1924 evolved into War Plan Orange—the blueprint for what eventually became the U.S. campaign against Japan from 1942 to 1945. Ellis envisioned a chain of assaults on heavily fortified Japanese bases across the Pacific, and through the 1920s and 1930s the Marines developed a series of new amphibious techniques and equipment. Despite all the pre-war work, the early assaults on Guadalcanal in 1942 and Tarawa in 1943 exposed serious flaws in the execution of the complex art of amphibious warfare. The Americans matured quickly, and the idea of "island-hopping"—bypassing and isolating heavily defended Japanese islands in favor of lesser targets—gained favor. The New Guinea campaign of 1943 and 1944 showed how well the United States was learning its amphibious lessons, leading to the great trans-Pacific invasions of 1944 and 1945, where immense armadas of ships unleashed swarms of Marines and soldiers on the Marianas, the Philippines, Iwo Jima, and Okinawa, and were poised by late 1945 to invade the Japanese home islands.

## 6. DIEPPE RAID (1942)

Looking to the future invasion of Nazi-occupied Europe, the British in mid-1942 felt the need to test their assault procedures and see how the Germans would react to an amphibious assault. The Soviets also were pressing for relief from the dormant Eastern Front. The small French port town of Dieppe was chosen as the site of the demonstration, and with the Canadian government pressing for more Canadian participation in the war, a force of 5,000 Canadians and about 1,000 British troops was formed. Rehearsals went poorly, the weather caused numerous delays, intelligence was bad, security was abysmal and some felt the entire operation should have been shelved. Unfortunately for most involved, it wasn't. In less than 12 hours of fiasco-packed action, more than two-thirds of the Canadian troops were killed, wounded or taken prisoner by the Germans. Allied troops and armor were cut to pieces on the beaches and reached few of their objectives. The British chiefs of staff found out the hard way they would need more and better air and sea support, and it was a tragedy so many died to find that out. There was one major benefit to the Allies from Dieppe. As astutely observed by British naval historian S. W. Roskill, "The Germans decided that the Dieppe raid indicated that, when the time came for the Allies to invade the European continent in earnest, their initial thrust would be aimed at capturing a large port. It is likely that this false deduction contributed greatly to the successful landing on the Normandy beaches in June 1944."

### 7. D-DAY: THE INVASION OF NORMANDY (1944)

Perhaps the best-remembered invasion in history, this giant operation on June 6, 1944, marked the return of Allied forces to Nazi-held Northern Europe. Politically and socially—particularly outside the Soviet Union—it marked the beginning of the end for Adolf Hitler, and the Germans surrendered nearly 11 months to the day after the "Great Crusade" set off by the invasion. American Gen. Dwight Eisenhower successfully balanced sensitive egos and blended a multi-national force into an unbeatable fighting team that, starting with 156,000 troops in northwestern France, would ultimately meet up with the Soviets in Germany. The subject of hundreds of books and films, "The Longest Day" even subsumed the generic term applied to all Allied invasions of World War II, where D-Day marked the first day of an invasion, just as H-Hour marked the time.

### 8. INVASION OF SAIPAN (1944)

As well-known as the invasion of Normandy remains today, it is almost forgotten that just over a week later, the United States pulled off another "D-Day" and sent a force nearly as large to invade Saipan, Guam, and Tinian in the Marianas Islands—a victory that emphatically led to the eventual end of the Japanese empire. That the United States could land 130,000 troops from several hundred ships in mid-Pacific simultaneously with the European assault remains one of the great military achievements of all time. The American invasion also called out the Japanese Fleet, jealously horded for most of 1943. The head-to-head fleet action, officially termed the Battle of the Marianas, is better known as the "Marianas Turkey Shoot" for the slaughter of poorly trained Japanese pilots. The loss of most of the Japanese Navy's carrier aircraft in this battle spelled an end to what, just over two years before, had been one of the world's crack military forces, and when the Japanese carriers reappeared in October 1944 during the invasion of Leyte Gulf, they were bereft of most of their combat aircraft and were used as decoy bait. The three main islands in the Marianas were transformed into bomber bases for the B-29 Superfortress to begin its assault on mainland Japan, and the planes that in August 1945 dropped the atomic bombs began their missions from Tinian. For this, more than 14,000 American troops, nearly 30,000 Japanese soldiers, and about 22,000 Japanese civilians were killed.

## 9. THE INVASION OF JAPAN (1945–1946)

The two largest amphibious assaults of World War II were cancelled by the August 1945 surrender of Japan. Having spent three years fighting its way across the Pacific, the United States was massing its forces for what both sides viewed as an epic and exceptionally costly struggle to end the war. As each succeeding U.S. invasion drew closer to the Japanese homeland, the intensity of the fighting and the level of casualties rose dramatically. Throughout the summer of 1945, U.S. invasion planners constantly revised upward their casualty estimates for the invasion of the home islands, and by early August were forecasting millions of Allied casualties with Japanese losses in the tens of millions—factors which played heavily on the minds of President Harry S. Truman and other U.S. leaders in their decision to use the atomic bomb on Japan. Operation Downfall was the overall plan to invade Japan and was split into two major parts: Operation Olympic, scheduled to invade the southernmost home island of Kyushu in November 1945; and Operation Coronet, planned to strike at the Kantô Plain near Tokyo, on the main island of Honshu in March 1946. The Japanese surrender on August 15, 1945, meant those landings never needed to be made.

## 10. INCHON LANDINGS (1950)

General of the Army Douglas MacArthur remains one of the great controversial figures of U.S. military history, alternately admired or reviled for many of the decisions he made during World War II, the post-war occupation of Japan, and in the Korean War. He conceived the invasion of Inchon and, against much professional opposition, championed and led its execution, which turned out to be a brilliant stroke of military leadership. With communist North Korea in control of nearly the entire Korean peninsula and threatening to completely kick out the United States and its allies, the invasion at this port city near Seoul reversed what had been an unending series of Communist successes, instead sending the United Nations forces northward in hot pursuit of the North Koreans. Ironically, as successful as the September 1950 invasion was, MacArthur exceeded his authority in chasing the communists north to the Chinese border and eventually provoked Red China into invading Korea. The Reds chased the allies again all the way down the peninsula before a counter-attack brought the front back nearly to where it all began in mid-1950, and President Truman fired MacArthur.

# Worst Peacetime Disasters

Had these disasters taken place during wartime their casualty totals would not have attracted great notice, but many of these events are better remembered than dozens of far worse wartime tragedies.

### 1. *BIRKENHEAD*
A British transport wrecked off South Africa on February 26, 1862, the *Birkenhead* sank with the loss of 445 troops and sailors.

### 2. *VICTORIA*
The British battleship *Victoria* sunk in collision with the battleship *Camperdown* off the Lebanese coast on June 22, 1893, with the loss of 358 officers and ratings—357 men were rescued. Vice-Adm. George Tyron remained on the bridge as the *Victoria* was sinking, and was heard to murmur, "It's all my fault."

### 3. *NIITAKA*
The Japanese cruiser *Niitaka* sank in a storm off Kamchatka on August 26, 1922, with the loss of 300 of her crew.

### 4. *LIBERTÉ*

The French battleship *Liberté* accidentally exploded at Toulon, France, on September 25, 1911, killing 285.

### 5. *MAINE*

The U.S. battleship *Maine* suffered an internal explosion on February 15, 1898, at Havana, Cuba, with the loss of 260 of her crew. Her loss was a major factor in the subsequent Span-ish-American conflict of 1898.

### 6. *OTVAZHNYI*

A Soviet destroyer of the Kashin class suffered an explosion, burned, and sank in the Black Sea on August 30, 1974, with the loss of more than 200 of her crew.

### 7. *HOBSON*

The USS *Hobson* (DMS 26), a U.S. destroyer-minesweeper, sank in collision with the carrier *Wasp* (CV 18) during night operations in the North Atlantic on April 26, 1952, killing 176 aboard the *Hobson*.

### 8. *BENNINGTON*

The USS *Bennington* (CVA 20) suffered a catapult explosion and fire at sea off Rhode Island on May 26, 1954. The aircraft carrier suffered 103 men killed.

### 9. *THRESHER*

The USS *Thresher* (SSN 593) was the world's first nuclear-propelled submarine to sink and, with 129 dead, remains the worst submarine disaster in history. She was lost while on post-overhaul trials on April 10, 1963, off the New England coast.

## 10. *KURSK*

The Russian nuclear-propelled, cruise missile submarine *Kursk*, lost after an internal torpedo explosion on August 12, 2000, in the Barents Sea, is the largest undersea craft to have ever sunk. One hundred eighteen men were lost with her, some remaining alive in an after compartment for several days.

# Worst Wartime Warship Disasters

These are the worst single-ship naval losses during wartime involving warships. Casualty figures in many cases are estimates.

### 1. PROVENCE
The French cruiser *Provence* was sunk by a German submarine in the Mediterranean on February 26, 1916, with the loss of 3,100 lives.

### 2. YAMATO
The Japanese super battleship *Yamato* was sunk on April 7, 1945, south of Japan by U.S. carrier aircraft with the loss of 2,498 officers and enlisted men.

### 3. HOOD
The large British battle cruiser *Hood* was sunk in the North Atlantic on May 24, 1941, by the German battleship *Bismarck* and heavy cruiser *Prinz Eugen*. There were three survivors from the *Hood*'s complement of 1,417 men.

### 4. *BISMARCK*

The German battleship *Bismarck* was sunk on May 27, 1941, in the eastern Atlantic. After being crippled by an attack of Swordfish torpedo planes from the British carrier *Ark Royal*, the *Bismarck* was sunk by British surface ships with the loss of 2,097 men.

### 5. *ROMA*

The Italian battleship *Roma*, en route to Malta as part of the Italian capitulation to the Allies, was sunk in the Mediterranean Sea on September 9, 1943, by a German air-launched glide bomb. The *Roma* went down with 1,352 of her crew.

### 6. *SCHARNHORST*

German battleship *Scharnhorst* was sunk by British warships on December 26, 1943, off North Cape, Norway, with the loss of 1,933 of her crew.

### 7. *TAIHO*

Japanese aircraft carrier *Taiho* was sunk by the U.S. submarine *Albacore* (SS 218) June 19, 1944, west of Guam, during the battle of the Marianas. The *Taiho* went down with 1,650 of her crew.

### 8. *FUSO* AND *YAMASHIRO*

The Japanese battleships *Fuso* and *Yamashiro* were sunk on October 25, 1944, in the Philippines by U.S. warships with the loss of more than 2,800 men. The *Fuso* and *Yamashiro* were among 14 Japanese ships that tried to force their way at night through the Suriago Strait to reach Leyte Gulf. American naval forces ambushed the Japanese ships and, in history's last battleship-versus-battleship duel, both Japanese dreadnoughts were sunk.

## 9. *SHINANO*

The Japanese aircraft carrier *Shinano*, converted during construction from a *Yamato*-class battleship, was sunk by the U.S. submarine *Archerfish* (SS 311) in Japanese coastal waters on November 29, 1944, killing 1,435 men.

## 10. *INDIANAPOLIS*

The worst U.S. naval disaster after the Pearl Harbor attack was the sinking of the heavy cruiser *Indianapolis* (CA 35) by the Japanese submarine *I-58* in the Philippine Sea on the night of July 29–30, 1945. The cruiser, which had just delivered atomic bomb components to the island of Tinian, had 1,196 men on board when she sank before being able to send out a distress message. About 300 men died when she sank; the survivors were adrift—on rafts and flotsam—for four days before they were rescued. Only 321 came out of the water alive, and four died a short time later; the others succumbed to thirst, exposure, and sharks.

# Worst Wartime Merchant Ship Disasters

A straightforward tally of wartime sinkings involving the greatest loss of life might cause surprise among many readers, who would find numerous large-scale disasters that today are nearly forgotten. The worst of these tragedies involved refugee, prisoner of war, and troop transport ships. Note the heavy losses among German passenger ships in the Baltic Sea, sunk as they evacuated troops and civilians from the advancing Soviet armies. All figures of those killed are estimates.

### 1. *LANCASTRIA*
This was a British troop transport, sunk on June 17, 1940, by German aircraft off the St. Nazaire, France. An estimated 4,000 people died, with some estimates running to 7,000.

### 2. *ARMENIA*
The *Armenia* was a Soviet hospital ship, sunk on November 7, 1941, by German aircraft in the Black Sea. More than 5,000 died, with some estimates running to 7,000 people.

### 3. *YOSHIDA MARU*

The *Yoshida Maru*, a Japanese transport, was sunk on April 26, 1944, in the Pacific by the U.S. submarine *Jack* (SS 259) with the loss of more than 3,000 troops.

### 4. *TOYAMA MARU*

The *Toyama Maru* was a Japanese transport, torpedoed on June 29, 1944, by the U.S. submarine *Sturgeon* (SS 187) with the loss of about 5,400, mostly Japanese troops.

### 5. *JUNYO MARU*

A Japanese transport, the *Junyo Maru* was sunk on September 18, 1944, by the British submarine *Tradewind* off the coast of Sumatra. At least 5,620 Allied prisoners of war and Javanese slave laborers were killed.

### 6. *WILHELM GUSTLOFF*

The *Wilhelm Gustloff* was a German refugee ship carrying civilians as well as troops. The ship was sunk on January 30, 1945, by the Soviet submarine *S-13*, in the Baltic Sea with the loss of up to 8,500 people. This was the worst disaster in naval history.

### 7. *GENERAL STEUBEN*

This German refugee ship, sunk on February 10, 1945, was also torpedoed by the Soviet submarine *S-13* in the Baltic Sea. She went down with at least 3,600 troops and refugees.

### 8. *GOYA*

A German refugee ship, the *Goya* was sunk on April 16, 1945, by the Soviet submarine *L-3* in the Baltic Sea. About 6,200 people were killed when she went down.

## 9. *CAP ARCONA*

Also a German refugee ship, the *Cap Arcona* was sunk on May 3, 1945, in the Baltic Sea by British aircraft with the loss of more than 4,200 people.

## 10. *THIELBECK*

The German refugee ship *Thielbeck* was sunk on May 3, 1945, in the Baltic Sea by British aircraft. More than 2,700 were lost with the ship.

# Television Series

The Navy as the setting for a television show has usually been a tough sell. Among the problems are how to depict seagoing life and the unfamiliarity of the public with nautical situations. In recent years the success of *JAG* and its stepchild *NCIS* has improved the situation, capitalizing on the current popularity of ensemble crime shows.

## 1. *VICTORY AT SEA* (NBC 1952–1953)

These 26 documentary-style episodes constitute one of the most important early television series, forever embedding in the minds of millions of Americans a vision of the U.S. Navy's role in World War II. Narrated by Leonard Graves, the series also featured stirring, original orchestral scores by composer Richard Rodgers.

## 2. *NCIS* (CBS 2003– )

Spun off *JAG*, this hour-long drama has done wonders to rehabilitate the image of the Naval Criminal Investigative Service. Special Agent Mark Harmon's eclectic team manages to routinely solve a variety of sophisticated crimes.

### 3. *JAG* (nBC 1995–1995, CBS 1997–2005)

This slick, well-produced show outlasted its critics and showed surprising resilience, even returning on rival network CBS after NBC canceled the show and it proved popular in reruns.

### 4. *MCHALE'S navy* (ABC 1962–1966)

This wild and crazy slapstick comedy played off the fame attached to President Kennedy's torpedo boat *PT-109*. Ernest Borgnine's Lt. Comdr. Quinton McHale (a lofty rank for such a lowly command) led a crew that included Tim Conway and Gavin MacLeod in a show that lasted longer than the World War II Pacific campaign it depicted. The show spawned two theatrical movies.

### 5. *VOYAGE TO THE BOTTOM OF THE SEA* (ABC 1964–1968)

Produced by the "Disaster Master" Irwin Allen, this science fiction thriller featured the nuclear submarine *Seaview* and a host of techno-wizthings. Richard Basehart starred as the admiral with David Hedison as the sub's skipper. The series was notable for beginning in black and white and switching to color for its second season. The show was the television version of the 1961 theatrical film.

### 6. *BAA BAA BLACK SHEEP* (nBC 1976–1978)

Based loosely on the adventures of legendary Marine Corps World War II ace Maj. Gregory "Pappy" Boyington, this series featured tough guy actor Robert Conrad leading a group of Marine fighter pilots at war with the Japanese and the military hierarchy. It also featured great aviation scenes with the F4U Corsair fighter plane.

### 7. *CPO SHARKEY* (nBC 1976–1978)

Conceived as a vehicle for comic Don Rickles—a Navy World War II veteran—this half-hour sitcom featured crusty, wisecracking Chief Petty Officer Otto Sharkey trying to deal with the new generation of sailors.

### 8. *NAVY LOG* (NBC 1955–1958)
The documentary-style *Navy Log* attempted to re-create some of the feeling of *Victory At Sea*. This effort expanded the historical scope to feature war stories from throughout the Navy's history.

### 9. *OPERATION PETTICOAT* (ABC 1977–1979)
A spinoff of the 1959 Blake Edwards film about a World War II U.S. Navy submarine and a group of nurses, this television series never really caught on despite featuring John Astin and Jamie Lee Curtis.

### 10. *THE WACKIEST SHIP IN THE ARMY* (NBC 1965–1966)
Another attempt to turn a modestly successful film into a television series, this sitcom about a spy-ship sailing vessel with Jack Warden and Gary Collins lasted only 29 episodes.

# Songs

There are thousands of Navy and sea songs that have come down through the ages. Vast numbers of these songs are rude, crude and downright dirty—sadly, those are not listed here. Here are ten of the better-known publicly acceptable ditties.

## 1. "ANCHORS AWAY"

The Navy's signature song came from a tradition begun by Naval Academy bandmaster Lt. Charles A. Zimmerman to compose a march each year for the school's graduating class. For the Class of 1907, "Zimmy" wrote the music and Midshipman 1/class Alfred Hart Miles penned the lyrics for what they thought would be just a football fight song. It was first performed on December 1, 1906, at the annual Army-Navy football game. While the song became universally recognized as the Navy's fight song, it has not been officially adapted as the Navy's service song.

## 2. "BELL BOTTOM TROUSERS"

This is a traditional ditty that dates from the 18th Century British Royal Navy, where it was known as the naughty shanty

"Rosemary Lane." Several dance orchestras recorded a safe-for-the-public version with words by Moe Jaffe in 1945 and the song gained widespread popularity.

### 3. "ETERПAL FATHER STROПG TO SAVE"

The Navy Hymn was written first as a poem in 1860 by Englishman William Whiting and set to music the following year by John B. Dykes. The hymn also is popular in Britain and France, and is widely associated with a number of seagoing tragedies. Numerous alternate lyrics have been written, including a 1955 version by George H. Jenks Jr. as "The Coast Guard Hymn."

### 4. "IП THE ПAVY"

This 1979 disco-flavored hit by The Village People— possibly the most successful pop song ever about the Navy—retains its staying power and continues to be widely played at Navy parties and in gyms.

### 5. "ПAVY BLUE AПD GOLD"

The Alma Mater of the United States Naval Academy was composed in 1923, with music by J. W. Crosley and lyrics by Roy DeS. Horn.

### 6. "POPEYE THE SAILOR MAП"

The cartoon sailor's theme song was written in 1933 by Sammy Lerner for the Popeye's first film appearance, in a "Betty Boop" cartoon. The infectious ditty with the unforgettable line, "I'm strong to the finich 'cause I eats my spinach" remains a classic, used in movies, television shows, and video games.

### 7. "PRAISE THE LORD AПD PASS THE AMMUПITIOП"

When the Japanese attacked Pearl Harbor on Sunday morning, December 7, 1941, a young chaplain aboard the heavy cruiser *New Orleans* (CA 32) did his best to keep up morale. Church services, of course, were not held while the battle was being fought, so Lt.(j.g.) Howell Forgy urged the men to "praise the Lord and pass the ammunition." After the battle, newspaper writers picked up the line and in 1942 composer and lyricist Frank Loesser turned it into a hit tune. Forgy at first preferred to remain anonymous, but in 1944 published his own account of the battle.

## 8. "THE REUBEN JAMES"

The sinking of the U.S. destroyer *Reuben James* (DD 245) by a German submarine shocked America in October 1941, and folk song artist Woody Guthrie thought the event should be commemorated in song. Guthrie quickly came up with a tune, but his first effort at the lyrics involved listing the names of all 86 men who died. His performing group, The Almanac Singers, wisely advised against such a long list. Group members Pete Seeger and Millard Lampell eventually came up with the chorus—"What were their names, tell me what were their names, did you have a friend on the good Reuben James?"—and a classic was born, memorializing not only the men of the destroyer but all men risking their lives at sea.

## 9. "SINK THE BISMARCK"

The 1960 movie *Sink The Bismarck* generated a new wave of interest in the 1941 saga of the German battleship, and later that year a popular song was released by Johnny Horton, who had something of a specialty in singing about historical events. Written by Horton and Tillman Franks, the song, with lyrics that were more catchy than accurate, topped out at No. 3 in the United States. The jacket for the 45-rpm single featured a picture of a battleship cut from the movie, but it was the wrong ship, depicting a model of the British *Prince of Wales*.

## 10. **"WHAT DO YOU DO WITH A DRUNKEN SAILOR"**

This British sea shanty dates at least from the early 19th Century. Reportedly based on a traditional Irish song, there are dozens (if not hundreds) of lyrics, most unprintable in a family publication. It remains perhaps the most recognizable sea shanty.

# Postage Stamps

Postage stamps help to reveal the culture of a nation and, for smaller countries, their economic prowess (selling commemoratives to foreign collectors). Many hundreds of stamps have been issued showing naval motifs—mostly warships. Here are some of the most interesting issues, both sets of stamps and individual stamps.

## 1. BACK HOME FOR KEEPS

Jon Whitcomb's portrait of a Navy lieutenant kissing his sweetheart was a 2001 stamp in the United States—and one of the authors' favorites. Whitcomb was a Navy artist in the Pacific during World War II and did the painting in 1943. Later U.S. postage stamps depicted the photograph of a sailor kissing a nurse in Times Square, New York.

## 2. SAILORS ON STAMPS

The 1945 U.S. stamp—all a shade of blue—shows ten sailors, part of a crowd of them, smiling up at the camera. The simplicity of this stamp makes it another one of the authors' favorites. A few Soviet stamps also showed sailors—almost always at war.

### 3. ADMIRALS ON STAMPS

Only a few admirals have appeared on postage stamps outside of the Soviet Union. The Soviet list is a long one. Adm.
P.S. Nakhimov was honored twice—in 1952 and 1954. Two
sets were particularly worthy of note: five admirals of previous centuries were honored in 1987 and six in 1989.

The father of the Russian Navy, Peter the Great, appeared
on an interesting stamp in 1971, showing him in a small boat
being rowed in a review of his fleet.

The United States issued a stamp in 1936 honoring Ad-
miral of the Navy George Dewey, the hero of the battle of
Manila Bay (1898). Of the four U.S. fleet admirals appointed
in 1944–1945, only one has appeared on a postage stamp:
Chester W. Nimitz in 1984. The great hero of the American
Navy, John Paul Jones, had his likeness on a 1936 stamp.
Jones served as an admiral in the Russian Navy.

### 4. NAVAL AIRCRAFT

The Curtiss *NC-4*, the first aircraft to span the Atlantic Ocean,
appears on the 4-cent stamp honoring Naval Aviation released
in 1961.

A 1996 U.S. postage sheet of 20 32-cent stamps shows
classic aircraft. Two naval aircraft are among the civil and military planes depicted—the Chance Vought F4U Corsair and
the Grumman F4F Wildcat. Also shown was the Boeing 314
Clipper flying boat. A similar 2004 sheet, with the U.S. basic
letter postage now 37 cents, shows only ten different planes,
with two Navy: the Consolidated PBY Catalina flying boat and
the Grumman F6F Hellcat fighter.

Several other nations have put a few aircraft on postage
stamps, but these sheets were the most impressive.

### 5. THE MORSKOY FLOTA

Russia probably receives the award for the most colorful "fleet"
of stamps. Several sets issued in the 1970s show an armada

of ships from the 1800s onward. The 1970 stamp showing the cruiser *Aurora*, which fired the (blank) shot that signaled the start of the Bolshevik takeover, is colored red. The *Aurora* also appeared on a stamp in 1988. Other ships of the 1970s sets included the helicopter-missile cruiser *Moskva* and a *Kashin*-class missile destroyer.

## 6. MARINE ITALIA
Detailed drawings adorn the beautiful stamps issued by Italy in the late 1970s and early 1980s, showing a variety of sail warships and modern ships and submarines. The sheets have beautiful maritime symbols in the margins of the sheets.

## 7. HISTORIC SHIPS
Sailing warships have adorned a couple of U.S. postage stamps. On the 150th anniversary of her launching (1947) the United States issued an attractive stamp showing the USS *Constitution*. A ship sometimes put forward as a near sister to the "Old Ironsides," the USS *Constellation,* was on a 2003 postage stamp. But that ship was actually a Civil War-built warship, the last sailing warship constructed in the United States. (Both ships are preserved.)

## 8. COMMEMORATING TRAFALGAR
In 2005—the bicentenary of the decisive battle of Trafalgar— the British post office issued a remarkable set of six stamps presenting two tableaus of the battle. One panel shows Lord Nelson, the hero of Trafalgar, being fatally wounded. A prestige stamp book also issued was lavishly illustrated and contained three White Ensign flag stamps and eight definitive stamps, as well as a text describing the battle and Nelson.

## 9. CIVIL WAR
More books and articles have been written about the American Civil War (1861–1865) than any other conflict involving

massive numbers of U.S. troops. But there have been few stamps commemorating events and people of that conflict. In 1994 the U.S. postal service did issue a 20-stamp sheet honoring battles and commanders (and a few others), including the battle of the *Monitor* and *Virginia* (neé *Merrimac*); the U.S. Navy's first (rear) admiral, David G. Farragut; and Confederate naval hero Raphael Semmes, who commanded the highly successful raider *Alabama*.

## 10. SUBMARINES

Many submarines have appeared on stamps from around the world. Probably the most depicted sub has been the USS *Nautilus* (SSN 571), the world's first nuclear-propelled vehicle. Among the more interesting U.S. *Nautilus* stamps was the "Arctic Exploration 1909–1959," showing an explorer's dogsled above the under-ice submarine.

The world's largest submarine—the Soviet Typhoon ballistic missile craft—has appeared on stamps from Russia (the first in 1996) to Guina-Bissau's 2001 issue. A 2005 issue by Russia provided views of six submarines—World War II-era craft up through (again) the Typhoon.

The "largest" submarine stamp was the 2000 issue of five attached stamps by the United States commemorating the first U.S. submarine, the *Holland* (SS 1). Also shown, each with a different domination, are an *S*-class sub, a World War II *Gato* (SS 212) class sub, an *Ohio* (SSBN 726) class "boomer," and a *Los Angeles* (SSN 688) class attack submarine.

The British postal service, a year later, published the centenary of the Royal Navy's submarine service with a less elaborate display of four stamps: the *Holland*, Britain's first submarine; the *Unity* class of 1939; the nuclear *Swiftsure* class of 1973; and the ballistic missile-armed *Vanguard* of 1992.

# More Quotations

We started with quotes, we'll end with quotes. Here are an additional ten quotations that the authors found interesting:

1. **THEY THAT GO DOWN TO THE SEA IN SHIPS, AND OCCUPY THEIR BUSINESS IN GREAT WATERS; THESE MEN SEE THE WORKS OF THE LORD, AND HIS WONDERS IN THE DEEP.**
Psalm CVII.

2. **A COLLISION AT SEA CAN RUIN YOUR ENTIRE DAY.**
Attributed to Thucydides (5th Century BCE).

3. **PLAY OUT THE GAME: THERE'S TIME FOR THAT AND TO BEAT THE SPANISH AFTER.**
Attributed to Sir Francis Drake (1588) when playing at long bowls on Plymouth Hoe, when reports reached him that the Spanish Armada was sighted.

4. **A MAN-OF-WAR IS THE BEST AMBASSADOR.**
Oliver Cromwell.

## 5. SHIPS IN THE HARBOR ARE SAFE, BUT THAT ISN'T WHAT SHIPS ARE MADE FOR.

Benjamin Franklin.

## 6. WHEREVER HIS FLEET CAN BE BROUGHT, NO OPPOSITION TO HIS LANDING CAN BE MADE. WE HAVE NOTHING TO OPPOSE HIS HEAVY GUNS.

Lt. Gen. Robert E. Lee.

## 7. ON LAND I AM A HERO; AT SEA, I AM A COWARD.

Adolf Hitler (1940).

## 8. PRAISE THE LORD AND PASS THE AMMUNITION.

Chaplain Lt. Howell Maurice Forgy serving on the heavy cruiser *New Orleans* (CA 32) during the Japanese attack on Pearl Harbor (1941).

## 9. TAKE HER DOWN.

Comdr. Howard W. Gilmore, severely wounded and unable to climb back into his submarine, the USS *Growler* (SS 215), in the face of approaching Japanese ships (1943). He was post-humously awarded the Medal of Honor.

## 10. THE NAVY IS A MACHINE INVENTED BY GENIUSES TO BE RUN BY IDIOTS.

Herman Wouk, *The Caine Mutiny* (1951).

# Bibliography

Bartlett, Merrill L., ed. *Assault From the Sea: Essays on the History of Amphibious Warfare*. Annapolis, MD: Naval Institute Press, 1983.

Brown, D. K. *The Grand Fleet: Warship Design and Development 1906–1922*. Annapolis, MD: Naval Institute Press, 1999.

Busch, Harald. *U-Boats at War*. New York: Ballantine, 1955.

Carpenter, Dorr, and Norman Polmar. *Submarines of the Imperial Japanese Navy*. Annapolis, MD: Naval Institute Press, 1986.

*Combat Fleets of the World* (biannual). Annapolis, MD: Naval Institute Press.

Elliott, Peter. *Allied Escort Ships of World War II: A Complete Survey*. Annapolis: Naval Institute Press, 1977.

Evans, David C., and Mark R. Peattie. *Kaigun: Strategy, Tactics, and Technology in the Imperial Japanese Navy 1887–1941*. Annapolis, MD: Naval Institute Press, 1997.

*Flottes de Combat* (biannual). Paris: Editions Maritimes.

Frank, Wolfgang. *The Sea Wolves: The Story of German U-Boats at War*. New York: Rinehart, 1955.

Friedman, Norman. *U.S. Aircraft Carriers: An Illustrated Design History*. Annapolis, MD: Naval Institute Press, 1983.

———. *U.S. Amphibious Ships and Craft: An Illustrated Design History*. Annapolis, MD: Naval Institute Press, 2002.

———. *U.S. Battleships: An Illustrated Design History*. Annapolis, MD: Naval Institute Press, 1985.

———. *U.S. Cruisers: An Illustrated Design History*. Annapolis, MD: Naval Institute Press, 1984.

———. *U.S. Destroyers: An Illustrated Design History*. Annapolis, MD: Naval Institute Press, 1982. (Revised Edition 2003)

Heinl, Robert Debs. *Soldiers of the Sea: The United States Marine Corps 1775–1962*. Baltimore, MD: Nautical and Aviation Publishing, 1991.

Hobbs, David. *Aircraft Carriers of the Royal and Commonwealth Navies*. London: Greenhill Books, 1996.

Hough, Richard. *Dreadnought: A History of the Modern Battleship*. New York: Macmillan, 1964.

*Jane's Fighting Ships* (annual). London: Jane's Publishing.

Jentschura, Hansgeorg, Dieter Jung, and Peter Mickel. *Warships of the Imperial Japanese Navy, 1869–1945*. Annapolis, MD: Naval Institute Press, 1977.

Kemp, Peter, ed. *The Oxford Companion to Ships and the Sea*. London: Oxford University Press, 1988.

Layman, R. D., and Stephen McLaughlin. *The Hybrid Warship: The Amalgamation of Big Guns and Aircraft*. Annapolis, MD: Naval Institute Press, 1991.

Lenton, H. T., and J. J. Colledge. *Warships of World War II*. Shepperton, Surrey: Ian Allan, 1973.

Love, Robert. *The Chiefs of Naval Operations*. Annapolis, MD: Naval Institute Press, 1980.

Lynch, Thomas G. *Canada's Flowers: History of the Corvettes of Canada*. Halifax: Nimbus Publishing, 1981.

Macintyre, Donald, and Basil W. Bathe. *Man-of-War: A History of the Combat Vessel*. New York: McGraw-Hill, 1969.

Marriot, Leo. *Treaty Cruisers: The First International Warship Building Competition*. Barnsley, UK: Pen & Sword Maritime, 2005.

Morison, Samuel Eliot. *History of United States Naval Operations in World War II*. 15 volumes. Edison, NJ: Castle Books, 2001 (reprint).

Morison, Samuel Loring, with Norman Polmar. *The American Battleship*. St. Paul, MN: MBI Publishing, 2003.

Muggenthaler, Karl August. *German Raiders of World War II*. London: Pan Books, 1980.

Naval Historical Center. *Dictionary of American Naval Fighting Ships*. 9 volumes. Washington, DC: Government Printing Office, various editions. Online at: www.history.navy.mil.

Parkes, Oscar. *British Battleships: A History of Design, Construction and Armament*. London: Hollin Street Press, 1957. (Reprinted 1973.)

Polmar, Norman. *Aircraft Carriers: A History of Carrier Aviation and Its Influence on World Events, 1909–1945*. Washington, DC: Potomac Books, 2006.

———. *Aircraft Carriers: A History of Carrier Aviation and Its Influence on World Events, 1946–2006*. Washington, DC: Potomac Books, 2008.

———. *Ships and Aircraft of the U.S. Fleet*. 18th edition. Annapolis, MD: Naval Institute Press, 2005.

Polmar, Norman, and K. J. Moore. *Cold War Submarines: The Design and Construction of U.S. and Soviet Submarines*. Washington, DC: Brassey's, Inc., 2004.

Reynolds, Clark G. *Famous American Admirals*. New York: Van Nostrand Reinhold, 1978.

Roskill, S. W. *The War at Sea 1939–1945*. 3 volumes. London: Her Majesty's Stationery Office, 1954–1961.

Silverstone, Paul H. *Civil War Navies 1855–1883*. New York: Routledge, 2006.

———. *The New Navy 1883–1922*. New York: Routledge, 2006.

———. *The Sailing Navy 1775–1854*. New York: Routledge, 2006.

Warner, Oliver. *Nelson's Battles*. New York: Macmillan, 1965.

# Index

# The Authors

**norman Polmar** is a leading expert on naval and aviation matters. Polmar has written more than 40 books, including the two-volume *Aircraft Carriers* and, with K. J. Moore, *Cold War Submarines: The Design and Construction of U.S. and Soviet Submarines*. He is also a columnist for the U.S. Naval Institute's *Proceedings* and *Naval History* magazines.

**christopher P. Cavas** is a senior correspondent for *Defense News*, former managing editor at *Navy Times*, and an expert on the Navy and its ships. Both authors live in the Washington, D.C., area.